Message In a Bottle
Geoffrey Richards

MESSAGE IN A BOTTLE

Observations from a Maine Bottle Hound

Geoffrey Richards

Quiet Waters Publications
Bolivar, Missouri
2006

Copyright ©2006. All rights reserved. Printed in the United States of America. No part of this book may be used or reproduced in any manner whatsoever without written permission except in the case of brief quotations embodied in critical articles and reviews.

Quiet Waters Publications
P.O. Box 34, Bolivar, MO 65613
E-mail: QWP@usa.net
For other titles, prices, and order information:
www.quietwaterspub.com

Photographs by
Geoffrey Richards and Lawrence Ronco

ISBN 1-931475-31-8
[ISBN 978-1-931475-31-0]

Library of Congress Control Number: 2005910908

ABOUT THE AUTHOR

Geoffrey Richards is a state of Maine man, having been brought up in the small community of Fairfield Center, Fairfield, Maine.

Geoffrey was a farm boy being raised in the country by his grandparents. At age 17, Geoffrey enlisted in the United States Marine Corps, serving in the Korean Conflict. Returning home after the conflict, he married Sandra Jones.

Geoffrey is a retired Superintendent of Schools. He spent thirty years in education; his life has been devoted to the educational development of children.

He received his Bachelor of Science degree from the University of Maine at Farmington in Science. His Master's of Education degree in Geography was also earned at the University of Maine at Farmington. He went on to the University of Maine at Orono, earning a second master's degree in Administration and in 1971 a certificate of advanced graduate study in Educational Administration. Dr. Richards earned his PhD in Educational Administration from Vanderbilt University, Nashville, Tennessee in 1980.

Dr. Richards has served as an Elementary Principal, a Secondary Principal, an Assistant Superintendent and a Superintendent of Schools, as well as having spent a number of years employed by the University of Maine at Farmington as a supervising teacher.

Dr. Richards is devoted to his wife, Sandra. Their family consists of a son, Nathan, his wife Kim, and three granddaughters, Heather, Kelsey, and Shannon. Over the years the family has enjoyed many adventures together. These adventures were mostly involved with hunting for and digging up antique bottles. This was both Dr. Richards' and his son Nathan's hobby. Many wonderful memories have been shared in this book.

Being devoted to his family, Dr. Richards firmly believes his hobby has bonded his family members closer together. Quality family time has been spent in the Maine wilderness, searching for old 18th and 19th century dumps and ultimately treasured bottles.

With this book, it is Dr. Richards' ultimate wish to generate an interest in others to venture out into Maine or elsewhere and develop a hobby.

Being a "bottle hound" is one proven way of bonding a family together. This can be especially difficult as we move into the millennium and the field of technology and communications becomes more time consuming.

Dr. Richards has shown a balance is necessary, both in his professional and personal life, a balance consisting of work and play. In work, his tools have been budgets, Boards of Education, and formal education. In play (being a bottle hound), his tools have been a potato digger, brush cutters, a camp saw, a spade, and a good pair of gloves. His hobby has benefited his profession by helping him to develop a healthy mind and at the same time helping to keep him physically fit.

Nathan and Kim Richards

INTRODUCTION

This book is not intended to be an accurate history lesson. The places described are real, and the author has incorporated them into the many adventures that are reflected in the contents. Should readers be inspired to read more about a given area, I refer them to their local library. My main concern in writing this book is to emphasize the joys of sharing personal experiences in the Maine woods. Adventures and treasures from Maine are still out there to be enjoyed by everyone. My wealth of knowledge came from simply using my senses to understand the natural world that surrounds each of us.

As the world and society have moved into the fast paced lane of technology, too often we have lost sight of what has made us a great nation. The advent of television, VCR's, and personal computers has helped to make many people sedentary. It's so easy to live for the moment, especially since breaking news is right at the turn of a knob. Most people live in a small world where their actions are dictated to them by this technology. We tend to forget the great happenings in our past that have helped to shape our destiny. Also, we appear to have forgotten the small pieces of history that have helped to shape our character.

Yes, I am talking about our heritage. I felt a need to look back to our early settlers and learn of their struggle. They had a burning desire to survive, and each member of a family had a critical role to perform.

In today's society, family members tend to go their separate ways. Very seldom do you see families enjoying themselves together. Too often families look to others outside of the family for their enjoyment. Years ago, in researching our genealogy, it appeared to me that the old cliché of "one for all and all for one," had never been so true. Families were very close; they had to be for survival.

This closeness appears to be missing in today's family. Fathers in their spare time are off playing golf, bowling, becoming members of a fraternal organization, or participating in a multitude of other activities. Mothers generally are involved in their own occupation and in outside activities associated with their colleagues. Many children appear to be left to "grow like Topsy." They find their own enjoyment. When their father is home, chances are he is parked in front of a TV, totally zoned out in sports. Their mother is often tired from her many duties; there is not enough energy left to share with the children.

Now, the children are the real losers in this society. They sit in front of their computers, living in a world far removed from personal contact with human beings. I am not being overly critical, and I am certainly not blaming the family members for their inactivity. They are active. This activity, however, is impersonal and directed toward inanimate objects.

This book is intended to help bring family members back together. it is intended to show family members that we, as human beings, can communicate without the use of today's technology. It's absolutely amazing how much closer my son and I have become over the years by being placed in situations where we had to communicate. One example will emphasize this bonding.

One day, he and I went on a bottle digging adventure. We were crossing in the middle of a river when the water began to rise. My son jumped safely to the closest side, and I, being too far out, could not make the jump. So I headed back toward the other bank. After several harrowing moments, I made it. I had to struggle in the river. The water tore off both of my sneakers, and I was desperate to survive.

This placed both of us on opposite sides of a raging river with several miles to go in order to walk back to civilization. We could not communicate as the roar of the river was too loud. We had to walk out on our own, each wondering if the other was okay. This was even more difficult as we were not familiar with the area.

We made it, though he was all bruised, and I was still in my stocking feet. Now, I do not recommend this extreme adventure for others to experience. Obviously, after he and I found out that each of us was okay, we had a grand time relating our experiences.

To this day, we share this great memory that could have been disastrous.

My point is, that fathers, mothers, sons, and daughters need to get off their comfortable duffs and start developing real life memories with each other. We cannot all become astronauts, scientists, Wall Street financiers, doctors, lawyers and so forth. If that's your desire then go for it!

However, the members of these demanding professions are also family members. I have often wondered what kind of family members these people are. Are they motivated by money, power or prestige? If the answer is yes, then we certainly need their expertise and our technology will continue to progress because of it. I hope, however, there are enough human emotions left in them to share with their families.

In writing this book, my motivation is that I want to share my experiences with others and to hopefully remind my readers of their human responsibility to the other members of their family. We are told that this is an era of communication. Yet in today's society, we have more lonely people then ever before. Families do not appear to communicate effectively and simply talking with each other seems to be considered out-dated.

My final wish in writing this book is to help families realize the bond that is created when the members of a family enjoy shared experiences. My life has been a joy thanks to the times I have shared with the members of my family. I wish the reader a happy life, and I'm thankful that others have allowed me to pursue mine. A part of my happy life has been shared in this book.

MESSAGE IN A BOTTLE

Early spring 1971 was the time when a great decision was made between my wife and I. We had contemplated whether to build or buy a camping place on a pond or lake that would be available throughout the winter months or to have an in-ground swimming pool installed in our backyard. We were thinking of making this decision in order to enable my wife and I and our young son to have some recreational activity that would be beneficial to each of us. We were a working family, and we needed some sort of activity we could do together as a family. The old adage that a family who works together, prays together and plays together was the driving influence in this great decision. The decision was finally made to install an in-ground swimming pool out behind our old shed and barn. We made the decision as a family, and we have never regretted eliminating deciding not to buy a camping place on some body of water away from home.

As a working family, both my wife and I were very tired when we both came home from work. We had just enough energy to pick up our young son, go home, and do all the things necessary to maintain a healthy lifestyle, including recreation or having fun as a family. Weekends were spent enjoying our son, and we did not feel like going off to camp, cleaning it, and doing all the other chores that go with camp life. Little did we know how this decision would influence the rest of our lives.

Now, it's appropriate at this time to enlighten readers as to one facet of my mind regarding the extended members of the family and their recreational fun or enjoyment. This enjoyment was the fun of hunting for or digging up old, antique bottles. Others in the family were having a wonderful time going on excursions in the countryside and bringing back these antique remnants of the past.

These years of enjoyment were primarily in the early and later 1960's. During these years, I was developing a career in education, and I found that I had little time for leisure. Therefore, I was not only uninterested in my family's bottle finds, but I actually laughed at great length on what they found, how they found it, the value of each bottle, and any anecdote surrounding their trip.

During these years there was also a tremendous interest by many people around the country to hunt for old bottles. It had been said that truckloads of these bottles were being transported out-of-state to antique dealers in the south and west. Many of these bottles were sold at auctions or to other bottle dealers. Other bottles were just collected as a hobby. This actually was a craze that developed for many people. Some people hunted for bottles for only their value. That is, a person would find a bottle, look up its value in bottle collectors' books, and then try to sell it for the listed price or whatever they could get for it. Money was their motivation. Others hunted for enjoyment, and made an excursion out of the hunt and enjoyed a picnic as a family while studying ancient cellar holes for relics. Some folks studied maps, talked to old-timers in the community, and walked for miles to locate old homesteads long since reverted back to nature. These persons eventually became local historians, archeologists, environmentalists, and then they finally developed an uncontrolled excitement—they became a fanatic "bottle hound."

Returning to the idea of the swimming pool out behind the shed and barn, we soon found that we felt something was missing. In the meantime, my son was now five years old and as a family we needed a place located by the pool where we could have fun. So, another family decision was made. We decided to convert the old shed into a family room—a *rumpus room* as it was finally called.

In the spring of 1971 the pool was completed and the work began on the shed. We were all excited about the construction; two old retired carpenters were hired to do the work. Our thoughts as a mom and dad of an energetic five year old were to create an environment where our son could enjoy playing with his friends.

Over the years, he would have a place to invite his school friends to come and swim, play music, dance, have parties, and do all the other things children do for enjoyment. Also, as a family, we could entertain friends and extended family.

During the construction of the rumpus room, an old outhouse was torn down. Little did we know that old outhouses would become of great interest to us in later years. Furthermore, our home was built during the early 19th century and reflected the *Big House, Little House, Back House* architectural design. Actually, according to records in the Somerset County Register of Deeds, our home was dated to ca. 1812. As a self-appointed US historian, I am well aware of the year's significance. During the War of 1812, our Capital was burned by the British, Madison was President, and his wife Dolly saved several historical pieces of art. I will not elaborate on history, but only mention the above to place your mind into the 19th century. Most of this book will concern itself with this period of time.

As work progressed on the rumpus room, a decision was made to not only tear down the "old three-holer" (backhouse), but also to install a sliding glass door. The day came to tear out the old doorframe where the sliding door was to be installed. The carpenters tore it out and hung an old drop cloth over the opening before going home for the night. During the process of this work, my wife and I would visit the construction site each evening and make decisions. These decisions were passed on to the carpenters the next day. This particular evening, I was looking over the door opening and was using my hand to feel behind the old beams. All of a sudden, I felt something tucked up behind a beam on the right side of the opening. It was a bottle! In fact it was a *Warner's Safe Cure for Kidney and Liver and Brights' Disease*. The bottle was in excellent condition, and it had its original label, and finding it sent me into a new dimension of excitement—bottle digging. For the next thirty years and even today, I have been and am a devout bottle digger. I am excited about every trip and about every bottle found whole or broken, and I find great joy in discussing all the facets of being a bottle hound with anyone who is willing to listen. Enjoyment is my motivator and a positive father/son relationship has been the result. A second generation, my son, has picked up the excitement and now asks me to go on trips with him. But, I am getting ahead of myself and must return to telling you about the bottle that changed my life.

Warner's Safe Cure for Kidney and Liver and Brights' Disease is considered to be primarily a patent medicine for women. I think the ingredients had a sizable portion of alcohol to cure disease. However, I will let you the reader be the judge. The label says it was to cure: "Brights' Disease, Jaundice, Gravel Stone, Catarrh of Bladder, pain in the Back, Headache, Dropsy, Impotency, Dyspepsia, inflammation of the Kidneys, Liver and Urinary Organs, tumors, Abscesses, Irregular Period, convulsions, female complaints, change of life. Beneficial in Gestation Disability, Malaria, Heart, Blood, Skin and other diseases caused by deranged Kidneys and Liver. Keep in a cool place and corked. Shake bottle well before using."

"Directions: Dose for adults. One tablespoonful six or eight times a day taken clear or in an equal amount of water, or in warm or cold milk before or after meals, to suit time or taste. If it nauseates, as it may in extreme cases, reduce the dose or heat it moderately and take after meals in warm or cold milk until the tone of the stomach is improved. For children under two years one teaspoonful, under 10, two teaspoonfuls warmed and taken in milk. Keep the bowels open of babies by injections, of children and adults by Warner's Safe Pills only. Discard all other medicine during treatment. Wear flannel or warm underclothing. Avoid all exposure and give the body a thorough rubbing once a day, taking care not to catch cold.

Diet In Extreme Cases: Diet is very important. Do not use fresh or salt meals or pork, spirits, beer, ice, water, tea, coffee, tobacco, hot bread, cakes, pies, pastry or any rich, greasy substances. Eat sparingly fresh fish, soft baked potatoes, soft boiled eggs, boiled onions, raw oysters, raw cabbage(both with but little vinegar), milk if agreeable, simple broths, corn and graham bread, tomatoes, asparagus, celery, fruits, moderately in seasons, if craved. Hot water, with simple fruit flavoring, should be drunk exclusively. For Diabetics use *Safe Diabetic Cure* only and *Diabetic Diet.*"

The cost of this amazing cure was $1.25 back in 1880, and it was manufactured by H.H Warner Co. Rochester, NY, USA, Toronto, Canada, and London, England. The bottle is amber in color, and it was made in a mold with an applied blob lip. It has an embossed safe on the backside with the words "Warner's Safe Kidney and Liver Cure" over the safe, and Rochester, NY embossed in the bottle at the bottom of the safe. There, as the reader, you be the judge. What were the ingredients? It sounds to me that, if you were sick, this tonic would either kill or cure. Certainly this medicine, along with others during this period in history, must helped to bring about "The Pure Food and Drug Laws" that protect our families today.

Now that I have elaborated on this most desirable and important bottle that changed my life, we must return to the swimming pool out behind the barn. As the pool people were digging the hole with a backhoe, several rusted, old tin cans, bottles, and other rubbish began to show up in the mound of dirt. In watching all of this, it dawned on me, they had dug into an old dump! "Hold it! Hold it!" I shouted and ran over to the debris. Lo and behold several bottles were unearthed. These were quickly seized and taken into possession. Much later I would find out these bottles were also used during the middle to late 19th century to hold household products or medicine. As you may think, my interest was again turning to excitement.

Finally, by the time the pool was completed, we decided (according to the law) that we would install a fence around the pool to keep children safe from this backyard body of water. I decided to put up my own fence, and I had it built in eight foot sections. To enclose the pool would take eighteen of these sections, along with two gates. The fence was six feet high, and each section was attached to posts embedded in the ground. Holes were dug and cement was used to stabilize the posts. Surprise, surprise, in digging the holes, I dug into two more dumps and more bottles were found. This discovery implanted in my mind that old-timers used to dig holes to bury their rubbish. This suggests that one of the first tools a bottle hound needs is a sounding rod. It should be metal, about five or six feet long and ½ inch to 1 inch in diameter. Over the years, this rod has been very handy in locating dumps and is best used in the spring of the year when the soil is soft.

By the time the pool, rumpus room, and fence were completed, I had found fifteen or twenty bottles of varied colors and uses. Being bitten by the bottle bug, I now began to dig holes all over my property with some results. I used the sounding rod, dug into banks, dug in depressions, and in general dug everywhere I thought there was a possible dump. My property soon looked like a big piece of Swiss cheese. Still my excitement was not satisfied, and I began looking inside my home behind boards, looking in the attic, cellar and back rooms. I found several more bottles of great interest—a *Rumford Chemical Works* blue bottle, a *Fellows Syrup of Hypophosphites*, a few amber medicine bottles, and one pottery cone ink well. By then I was delirious and overcome by excitement, and I could not seem to stop thinking of all the old bottles out there somewhere, waiting to be found. Might I add, these bottles that I found in and around my home are minor treasures compared to what my son found in and around his home (circa 1786) in the year 1997. But once again, I am getting ahead of myself and must return to the early 1970's.

Remember how had I laughed at members of my extended family for being interested in digging for old bottles? Well, now I had to eat crow. Family members wondered what was going on when I said things like, "What a terrific find! Have you located that bottle in a book? Where did you find it? Can I hold it? Look at it?" My interest was really coming through. My mind was eating up everything being said, and I was learning new things all over again. This was knowledge outside the professional career to which I had devoted my life. It was truly fun to learn new terms or a vocabulary generally known only to bottle diggers. Terms like: pontil, blob top, applied top, three piece mold, automatic bottle machine, *Kovels Bottle Books*, *American Bottle Collectors Association*, torpedo bottles, fire extinguisher grenades, household bottles, medicine bottles, misc. bottles, ink bottles, and poison bottles to name a few of the terms. But what really blew my families' mind was when, tongue and cheek, I asked if I could go along on their next excursion. A few choice words were directed at me, but in the end my family forgave me and welcomed me into their bottle digging inner circle. I had apologized and now had someone to talk with about my new found hobby. Sharing stories, adventures, bottle knowledge, excitement, and family enjoyment became all important to this bottle enthusiast.

Preceding my crow-eating apology, I remember vividly a visit my wife and I had with other family members to a pond in Oakland, Maine. During our visit, my brother-in-law and another person walked up an old road, located an old dump, and brought back several pails full of old bottles. As I remember, I was not impressed at the time as bottles were then not my thing. But I never forgot the visit and the general location of the dump. Sooooo! You guessed it. When I had time after I became interested in bottle digging, I went looking for the dump in Oakland and found it. It was a rock pile that had been dumped over old bottles and other trash dating to the late 1800's. It was beside the road leading down to camps located on the pond. I began to dig with my hands, moving rocks and other old material that had grown or gathered over the rocks and bottles.

It must be pointed out at this time that an aroma permeates your nose from the earth. Over the years of digging, this aroma appears to always be present in old dumps. It is not an objectionable odor. In fact it is a musty, earthy smell that is released from underneath the first layer of moss, rocks, earth, etc. that cover the old dump. I find the aroma very pleasant as it is part of the environment. Other tell-tale signs of an old dump are prevalent. For example, depending on the time of year, the pesky black flies, mosquitoes, and other insects add another problem to all the others that a bottle hound must deal with. The structure of the earth the dump is found in can also be a problem. This particular dump in Oakland was over and under a rock pile. Other dumps can be found behind rock walls or deep in the earth located by a depression in the lay of the land. Hillsides, ditches, cellar holes, and outhouses are still other sites for dumps. As we talk about other bottle digging adventures that my family and I went on, I will briefly describe the environment as each dump has its own charm. All you must do is first smell the ever-present earthy odor and then you are aware of your surroundings.

As I dug in the Oakland dump, I began to find all sorts of treasures, such as old whiskey bottles from *Hayners* and plain quart size black glass unembossed bottles were found. Many medicine and household bottles were also discovered of different shapes and sizes.

The difference between the words *embossed* versus *unembossed* needs to be explained. *Embossed* is a term used to describe any lettering, figures, or pictures found in the glass of a given bottle. The mold in which the bottle was blown had the embossing made right in its structure, so that when the bottle was finally taken out of the mold, you could visualize exactly what the bottle was intended for. You could read about its contents, when and where it was made, who made it, and any other information the owner wanted you to know. *Unembossed* simply meant the bottle was clear or colored with no markings other than the seams of the mold.

I spent the day in Oakland enjoying myself and gathering all sorts of old, antique bottles. How I wished my son had been with me. It was a pleasant dump overhung with tree limbs. Bushes grew up through the rocks, and back over the down slope was a wet hole used by a family of frogs. The wet hole also served as a breeding ground for insects. I watched closely as a snake slithered in and out of the rock pile. The sun was out, birds were singing, and as I worked the shade provided coolness to dry off my perspiration. Every find created excitement. How I wished I could share this excitement with someone. It finally dawned on me: for Lords' sake take your treasures, go home, and return with your son! There was still plenty of daylight left, and that was exactly what I did.

My son was not into bottle digging, nor was he yet bitten by the excitement the way I had been bitten. He was still a very small boy of five or six years old. However, I was determined to share this excitement. Of course, I was hoping my son would become my sidekick as I traveled the countryside looking for old dumps. Nothing would be greater than to introduce this small boy to the wonders of nature through this hobby. Little did I know he was at a very impressionable age and learning came quickly and easily to his eager mind. (As a point of interest and after many years of bottle digging, with my son now grown into manhood, this desire to instill nature into this once small boy has paid dividends. He now has a greater desire than I to travel the backwoods and hunt for old 18th and 19th century dumps. He is a self-anointed archaeologist, environmentalist, history buff, and naturalist. In summary, I think he is a very wealthy man who is motivated by the enjoyment of being with and being a part of nature—all this through digging for old bottles.)

It was late afternoon when we returned to Oakland and began to dig. Again, we turned up old beer bottles, more whiskies and miscellaneous others. I always showed my excitement and tried to instill this into my son. He was busily digging, removing rocks, and in general, for his size, working as hard as I was working. Shoulder to shoulder we had started on the backside of the dump by the wet hole and slowly worked our way back toward the pond road. As we got closer to the road there was a line of bushes. Moving even closer there was one exceptionally large bush, about 3" in diameter, slanting back over our heads. I was digging to the left of the bush and my son was directly in front of its stump. His digger struck glass as he prodded beneath the stump.

The sun was over our shoulders and illuminated the hole he had created. My attention was immediate as the clinking sound was made between metal and glass: The tell-tale sign of a possible bottle. I could see something resembling an old bottle, but it was a new find even for me. My son reached under the bush and pulled out his first find. It was an excellent, old case gin bottle, tapered with ridges running the full length like lines or shingles, with a blob top and dark green in color. As he held it up, his first treasure, I began to holler, "Super! Super! What a find!" I am sure he thought I had lost my senses, but since I was his father, he just looked at me in amazement. We both shared in this excitement and held this case gin for several minutes, passing it back and forth to study and feel its shape. I am convinced that this antique bottle called a case gin and its find was the moment in time, shared by father and son, that cemented or bonded a lasting love for digging old bottles. it also created a friendship between us that grew into a common thread that ran so true throughout many, many years.

It was getting late, and we had to pick up our considerable treasures. Placing them in several old, rusty buckets, we walked through the shadowed figures that danced in the woods and fields from the setting sun and went home. Onward we went, as the old-timers used to say, "heading the horse toward the barn." We were weary, dirty, lame, and bruised, with one finger cut, but we were also filled with joy as we traveled and talked all the way home.

We returned to this dump several times in later years and were never disappointed. The last time we ventured to Oakland and its hidden dump, we were somewhat destructive, and I am reluctant to say that the dump continued underneath the road leading to the camps. We dug a small portion of the roadbed away. To this day, that roadway still covers part of that dump. If the road is ever discontinued, I am sure my son will be the first bottle digger to be on the spot. For interest's sake, we found out in later years this dump was used by an old tavern. It was built on a hill a few hundred yards away, across the road and up over a hill in a large field long since allowed to go back to nature. The foundation of the tavern is still located in this field.

Before leaving this wonderful dump, I feel obligated to relate another memory. As we dug away portions of this roadbed, we had to listen for cars coming and melt away into the woods as they got nearer and finally passed our spot. Coming toward and going away from the area, the roadbed was probably ten feet wide, with ditches on both sides. At the site where we were digging, there was no ditch and approximately six or seven feet of gravel bed left. I am sure the Lake or Pond Association had to have gravel hauled in to fill our excavation.

For those of you who have never experienced blisters on your hands and the soreness of bruised fingers, or even bloodied cuts, bottle digging is for you. That is if it doesn't bother you to get your hands dirty. This hobby (that's what we call it) goes hand and hand with dirty, hard work. Tools used in the digging process can vary depending on the size, location, and make-up of the dump. Spades, rakes, forks, bow saws, bush cutters, axes, hand tools like hammers etc., or even pick axes are all used—although I will never use a pick ax again. Many years into digging, I used one to loosen some dirt that was as hard as clay. Deep into the bowels of a dump, I struck a pail. The pick went through the pail and broke a beautiful old bitters bottle that was inside the pail. To this day, I remain sad, especially since my son advised me at the time not to be so rough in my digging. It would be just super if a bottle digger could use a gas powered backhoe or a small gas or diesel bulldozer, but we are not that lucky, and the other tools mentioned are still the cornerstone of moving earth or rocks for the bottle hound. Crowbars, levers, potato diggers, and just brute strength appear to be the only safe methods to move or rearrange dumps. Indeed, when you look at a site that has been dug using only these small hand tools diligently in an old dump, it really looks like a bulldozer has been used. One can destroy many bushes and trees, move tons of rock and dirt, and dig serious holes (very deep) with these implements. Standing back after a long day of digging and looking over a dump, it sometimes looks like a road crew with heavy equipment has excavated a site.

A rule of thumb to use in selecting tools to dig bottles is to use anything that will move earth or rocks without damaging the bottles located in the earth and under the rocks. I remember my son using a winch to move rocks in an old cellar hole. The winch was attached to an old 1975 Land Cruiser, and it worked great. He would wind the cable around a foundation stone and lift loosened stones that were pried out with a crowbar. As I recall, he found several old, valuable bottles then. But by far the best tools are your hands, covered with a good pair of gloves, and a potato digger. Some bottle hounds use metal detectors to locate old dumps. Old metal pails, tin cans, parts of old wagons and horseshoes can help find the location of some old dumps when you use the detector. Generally, wherever you find old metal you will locate glass.

One beautiful, sunny, Saturday morning my stepfather-in-law and young son started out for the little village of Larone, Maine. The village was located just a few miles from our home and had a local history that included being settled around 1788. This particular date suggested that the sites of old homes could most likely be found along a stream known as Martin Stream. An old granite dam had been built for a sawmill and a grist mill along its banks. Neither of these mills was still in existence.

That day we decided to start our dump hunting down by the dam. We walked down through bramble bushes and blackberry bushes and found the rotted remains of an old sawmill that had used the dam for waterpower. It had long since gone into disrepair and probably was closed in the 1930's. We kept on walking and crossed over mounds of sawdust covered with honeysuckle bushes, shrubs, and trees growing up through the sawdust. The sawdust was old and had blackened over the years.

Just beyond these sawdust piles was a flat area where the stream had eroded away the banks. Further to the right was a steep slope covered with huge boulders. These boulders were dumped there to cover an old dump filled with glass, tin cans and other items that had been of no use to the owner.

Our first inkling that it was a dump of value came when we saw old broken bottles, blob tops, crockery, and the ever present iron metal sticking out of the ground. We all began to dig in this area that had been eroded away by the stream.

Yes, we began to find things, but something happened to stop each of us in our tracks. My son stepped on some broken glass and cut his ankle. It was not a serious cut, but it bled continuously. He did not want to stop digging until his grandfather assured him that we would return another day. With that assurance, grandfather picked up my son and carried him in his arms back to the car.

This incident ended the trip, but it also brought us closer together as a family. It became an adventure that we never forgot. My son was not hurt seriously, and we did return several times to dig for old bottles and were successful. Nathan still bears the scar from that day on his right ankle.

On one such trip back to this dump, we took a picnic lunch. After digging for several hours and having little luck, other than finding a lot of old broken glass and some minor small bottles, we sat down to eat our lunch in the same location my son had been cut on the previous trip. As we were eating, Nathan spotted the neck of an old bottle sticking out of the dirt and hard sand that had been left there by the receding water of the stream. He reached down, pulled on the neck, and out popped an old round-bottomed torpedo bottle, blob topped, Vincent Hathaway ginger ale bottle that was embossed with the location Boston, MA.

What luck! We were beginning to build a collection of old, antique bottles that were becoming our pride and joy. As the reader might imagine, excitement was crackling between father and son. If you find one bottle there must be others. Also, finding that one bottle sent our adrenaline soaring. This renewed energy created strength we did not know existed. Great boulders were rolled away, dirt was flying, and bushes and small trees were easily pulled out by the roots. A bite from an insect was not felt, and the time of day flew by, until we realized that the sun had gone down and we had better get for home with our treasures.

One might observe that it takes great strength, agility, and all the other physical qualities to dig bottles. Along with these qualities, perseverance and stamina are equally important. Actually a healthy, strong body is a requirement for success as a bottle hound. Sometimes brute physical strength is the only way to reach that particular bottle you know is hidden between two boulders or beneath a large bush, especially when you do not have the proper tools.

When you walk onto an old dump, the first task is to size up the necessary work to uncover the treasures. In cruising the backwoods, tote roads, lumber camps, discontinued country roads, and old settlements, looking for dumps, usually one travels light. However, should you be lucky enough to know the kind of dump for which you are looking, probably you have brought the right implements. If you do not know, chances are your physical strength and whatever you can find for tools will prevail, such as an old iron rod lying in the dump that will become your digger. A broken limb will make you a lever to move rocks. I think you get the idea.

If you're way back in the woods and come across an old dump, the excitement of finding that special bottle drives a true bottle hound to reinvent the wheel. Particularly if the only implement available to you is your body and your good old Maine or Yankee ingenuity. Certainly, should a return trip be in the back of your mind, you would then know what to take for tools to make your adventure more productive.

It is only proper at this time to make budding bottle hounds aware of the possibility of failing to find a dump, let alone a bottle. My son, friends of ours, and I have tramped the backwoods, ghost towns, and even walked present day roadways looking for dumps to no avail. I am sure we have logged miles and miles without finding a single thing. A true bottle hound simply chalks these miles up to part of the hobby. Might I add, even these trips can be enjoyable. It is fun to turn the trip into a nature walk, animal, or bird watching excursion, or have it become simply a healthy walk for physical activity. As I have said, if your motivator is enjoyment, then enjoy your adventure.

I am lucky, as I have a geographic and physiographic (study of glaciations) background. It is not necessary to have this sort of background, but it helps me in this way: I can locate a high spot on my walk and climb to the top of a hill, mountain, or whatever the elevation. Once there, I simply sit down and observe the landscape. Usually, old tote roads become visible; valleys, gullies, bodies of water also become more prominent.

I can then begin to piece together what the landscape looked like a couple of hundred years ago. It is amazing how old apple trees can stand out in an old field that has gone back to nature, or how easy it can be to see old maple trees that were once used for a family's sugar. Obviously, the old apple trees and old sugar maples were planted by past generations.

Old cemeteries and bridges that once helped people cross bodies of water can also be seen by the naked eye. It would not hurt to have a pair of binoculars to help the vision. Even more specifically, when you find an old foundation, you can usually locate the cellar entrance or bulkhead. This exit from the cellar is where the occupants perhaps loaded the old wagon with trash to haul to the dump. Usually, the horses were turned downhill to haul the wagon that was heavy with trash. So, look for gullies or fields downhill from the house. A gully behind an old home is usually a dead giveaway for the dump.

The far end of a field is also a likely spot. At the end of the field always look for exceptionally large trees in a clump compared to their surroundings, this is another give away.

By far the greatest dump locators are stone walls. They provide a maze blocking off fields, lanes, and pastures. Walking these old stone walls can be very rewarding. Look for openings in the walls where the owners' wagon could have passed through on its way to the "back forty." Locate well holes, old sheds, and back-houses. I can just picture an old timer sitting on his one, two, or three–holer after a hard days work. Perhaps he is drinking some old cider out of a crock jug, whiskey out of an old black glass bottle, or even an historical flask, then unaware of its value, tossing the container down the hole beside him. Many a valuable bottle has been found in the ancient bedding of old outhouses.

Another sure way to locate a dump is to find the backdoor of the kitchen area or where you think it might have been. Stand in that spot and scan the backyard. Look for depressions or hummocks that appear not to be natural. These areas would be great places to use a sounding rod. The housekeeper probably hung out clothes by exiting through this door. Children may have played in the backyard. The back kitchen door is a good place to start your hunt for old dumps.

Turn your trip into a treasure hunt using all of your senses, and you will be amazed at the results. You may not locate a dump or find a bottle, but with these ideas, and the ones you may come up with on your own, a great adventure can be yours.

To help you to be more successful, go to the County Registry of Deeds. Ask for copies of old maps that will trace discontinued country roads, old villages, and abandoned neighborhoods. These maps are a must in order for you to be on top of your hobby.

Another trip that my son and I took was on the old Airport Road in Norridgewock, Maine. An old cellar hole was known to exist out by the Sandy River in

Norridgewock. It was easy to find, and I assumed we would find nothing at the site as it was beside the road. The buildings had burned, and the only thing left to indicate it was a dwelling was where trees were growing up through the cellar hole.

It was another beautiful day, and the old foundation was in the middle of a field overlooking a portion of the Sandy River Valley. We parked the car, got out our potato diggers, and walked to the site. We then began to dig. After a period of time we realized most of the trash we were turning over could be dated to about the 1930's and 40's.

In the middle of the cellar hole was an old spring mattress. My son moved the mattress and uncovered a quart size, peacock blue, wine bottle. It had bubbles all through the glass, and we considered it a terrific find to add to our collection.

In moving the old metal spring once more, my son drove a spring into his knee and that ended our adventure. He was not hurt seriously, but we drove home after administering first aid. I still have this bottle and the interesting memory it radiates each time I look at its beautiful color. This short trip reminds me to relate to readers and would-be bottle hounds the absolute necessity of taking a first aid kit on any and all excursions into the field. Today, someone has built their home directly over the cellar hole, thus eliminating all traces of past generations.

Bottles are not the only treasures found in old dumps. Ox yokes, wagon wheels, old chicken and turkey weights, foot scrapers, copper pails, three-tined forks, whiffle trees, and old miscellaneous farm tools are also treasures to be brought home to be admired and displayed.

Once, when my son and I were out in the town of Starks, Maine, we came across the remnants of an old sugar shack. It had all fallen down. We commenced to kick around in the dead leaves and began to find old spiles dated from the 1860's to 1897. These were used to tap the maple trees for syrup. I have a display of these spiles in my home. In today's world of maple syrup, plastic spikes and plastic tubing are used to harvest the sap from sugar maples. These old metal spiles have passed into oblivion and now are considered antiques.

Old lanterns are another treasure waiting to be unearthed as are keys, marbles, and coins. One never knows what will be found when digging in an old 19th century dump. This helps add to the excitement of the search and keeps the bottle hound deeply interested in his hobby.

Sandwiched in-between the younger years of my son's life were many jaunts into the Maine woods. We were always entertained by Mother Nature, and our interest continued to grow with our hobby. On one such excursion, we had traveled to Bingham, Maine and were on the backside of Baker Mountain. We had stopped by an old cellar hole, taken out our trusty diggers, and walked out behind the site.

Traveling out in the woods we became separated. As I studied the terrain, a bull moose was studying me. All of a sudden, I was very close to the bull and hollered to my son. I did not know where he was located in relation to the moose or to me. He answered from a short distance away. But, when I yelled, the bull moose started running, making one heck of a noise. I yelled again and said something like, "Watch out, here he comes!" and with that alarm the moose ran directly between us and as far as I know he is still running.

This encounter left both of us a little rattled, very excited, and more than ready to leave the area. It was a valuable experience and a terrific memory. I remember that it was in the fall of the year or late summer because the leaves were turning.

As we left the site, the roadway began to run parallel with a small brook. It was a beautiful brook and took our eye. So we stopped and walked down over the bank and up the brook. I came to a clear pool of water and swimming around in this pool were several good-sized brook trout. This sight was "gravy for the potato": Meaning although we found no bottles, once again Mother Nature did not let us down. Fish will congregate in deeper pools in the fall to help them keep cooler.

The pool became a mini spring hole. I sat down among the spruce-fir and hemlock, and enjoyed the coolness of the forest as I listened to a red squirrel scolding me. This was relaxation that can only be found in the forest. Many times I have experienced the wonders that Henry David Thoreau writes about in his travels through Maine in the mid 1800's. No wonder he wrote about Walden Pond and secluded himself in a small cabin for two years.

On other trips I have startled deer with their telltale white flag waving at me as they moved to quieter spots in the forest. I have watched bald eagles soaring in the updrafts over the Kennebec River from Moosehead Lake to Sidney, Maine. On one occasion below Indian Dam, around Moxie Falls in the Kennebec River, a family of otters was out for an early morning hunt. It was very early and I was searching the upper river bank for remnants of the river drive that ceased in 1976. I was on one side of the river, and the otters were on the other side.

As I watched and listened to their squeaks and familiar guttural sounds, one of the otters spotted me and came slithering down over the rocks into the water and swam directly toward me. As he came closer, he began to hiss at me and swam in circles for a couple of minutes before returning to his family. What a joy to see this display of dissatisfaction with my presence in their territory.

By the way, on an island in the middle of the river, I found an old, pearl-handled knife that was stuck in a hemlock tree about 8 feet high. I took a long branch and knocked it down. Yes, I still have the knife, and I like to think it was driven into that tree by a burly, old lumberjack riding the logs down the river during the log driving days.

On another occasion, in the town of Starks, I was alone and searching for an old foundation along a discontinued county road. I had an old map of the area and was estimating the distance I would have to travel, which was considerable. The general direction was in the northwest corner of the town on the Somerset and Franklin County lines. The roadbed led north toward the town of Industry.

I began to trudge along the washed out, gravel roadbed. As I walked, the road began to slope down a long hill. The area had been cut over by logging operations. I came across a couple of old hovels where horses were sheltered. Continuing on down the hill that was closely bordered with alder, birch, poplar, and 3rd growth hardwood, the roadbed began to disappear into a large bog area. Alders took over my path as I forced myself forward toward an opening.

Breaking into the opening, I found myself standing on the south end of an enormous beaver dam. The dam appeared to run north in the general direction of the road. Indeed, the energetic beavers had built the dam directly on top of the road. Continuing on, I observed a huge beaver house. The dam was approximately 50 yards long and as much a 6' high in certain places. This dam actually covered the entire distance across the valley floor.

Starting up the other side of the valley, the road became much easier to walk. I passed beneath some high tension lines as I walked steadily up a steep grade, eventually nosing myself into an old field. The steepness of the roadbed amazed me, and I wondered if someone did live here during the middle to late 1800's.

"How did they manage to get to town?" I wondered. Certainly it was by horse and buggy, or wagon maybe drawn by oxen. At any rate the traveling must have been superhuman. "How did the children get to school?" I also asked myself. Maybe they did not go to school, maybe they were just taught the necessities at home.

After plodding along for three or four miles I came upon several maple trees lining the roadbed. My heart began to beat a little faster as it always does when the excitement starts in my mind at the possibility of locating a dump. Might I add, this physical excitement has been called, "smelling the bottles out." My son was not with me, but I swear he has a great nose for smelling out dumps.

As I continued to walk, I noticed that the roadbed leveled out, and I found myself on a high ridge. Turning around and looking back, I was amazed to see a most beautiful, panoramic view of the valley and the surrounding wilderness. Not a single human cultural object was in sight. It quickly became obvious to me why a man would build his home in this location.

As I observed the view, my hearing seemed to become more acute, my sight more vivid, and my smell very pronounced. My senses were telling me something was about to happen. Sure enough, the remnants of an old house came into view with an attached shed and barn. The same old, New England architectural design I referred to before as, "Big House, Little House, Backhouse, Barn."

I stood in awe looking at the fallen down structure and studying the surroundings. A family of porcupines had taken over sections of the old barn, and burdocks had grown around the foundation and front entrance of the house. In back of the house were the remnants of old apple trees and an old tote road leading down toward a rock wall.

As I walked slowly down the tote road, the rock wall gave way to an opening. Passing through the opening and looking to my left, I came upon the most beautiful dump spread out over the top of the ground. It was covered with old leaves, moss, and pine needles dropped from one old, lonely, scrub pine.

I dropped to my knees and furiously began to dig and scrape. I unearthed bottle after bottle. They were old and dated back 100 years. A few were sun colored and amethyst, many were bottle glass green and amber, some were clear, and a couple were blue. All these bottles had bubbles in the glass, and two had pontils.

It seems that, when you find bottles, your energy is heightened. I dug and searched well into the late afternoon. When the sun began to sink lower in the sky, I felt the dump was pretty much cleaned out, and I started to gather my thoughts. I was thinking, for example, how would I get all these treasures out to where I had parked the car several miles away?

Filling every pocket and several old pails with my bottles, I started back along the old roadbed and down the hill, under the power lines and toward the

Beaver Dam. Along the way back I came across a ravine and to my amazement spotted another dump. It was very late, the sun was just about ready to set, and I was tired. To this day, I have no idea where my energy came from.

As I put my heavy load down and slipped and slid down over the bank of the gully, sure enough I found more bottles of many descriptions and sizes. There were medicine bottles, household use bottles, old canning jars, and soda bottles, along with a smattering of others. Upon the road, I already had about fifty bottles, and that was more than enough for me to have to carry. What would I do with another forty or fifty bottles, especially with a couple more miles to walk?

By this time the sun was just about set. I decided that, if I walked fast, I could make two trips. I knew full well it would be very dark by the time I finished. So to make a long story short, I did make two trips and came out with more than 100 old bottles. I have since returned to this location. The beaver dam is still there, and I can still picture the old farmhouse and often think of the family living on that high ridge, and how they must have struggled to live in such a remote place. I am sure those folks were strong, independent, and self-reliant, and that they lived a life of joy and happiness—at least that is the memory I have of this terrific trip into the wilderness of Starks, Maine.

On another trip to Starks, in a different location, I traveled up Mayhew Road toward Mount Hunger.

My son was with me, and we parked close to Ditson Cemetery. Perhaps one would wonder, why I was so interest in Starks? Well, I call this area Brackett Mountain. Two of my great, great uncles and my great, great-grandfather lived on this mountain, and their last name was Brackett. My middle name is Brackett and my relatives on my father's side came off the top of this secluded place. My great great-grandfather, Orlando, had several children, one of which was Charles Brackett, my great-grandfather. He in turn moved down to Starks Village and became a blacksmith and furniture maker. Charles had several children, one of which was my grandmother, Mable Brackett. Mable became a school teacher, married John Richards from Farmington and had one son, my father, Roger Richards. Enough of this genealogy; let us continue this trip up Hunger Mountain, which I knew as Brackett Mountain.

Ditson Cemetery has just a few gravestones. As we approached, it became apparent these pioneers lived in the early part of the 19th century. It amazed us to find a cemetery surrounded with a white fence and an American Flag adorning one of the graves. This cemetery could easily be missed unless you knew it was there. I am assuming the town of Starks decorates and maintains this secluded spot. What a wonderful feeling to know the people of Starks care about these early inhabitants.

As we began to ascend the mountain, we passed an old gravel pit and found ourselves in the middle of a wide lane. The lane was probably ten yards wide and bordered on both sides with a rock wall. These rocks were meticulously placed and created a four-foot high barrier. Looking at these stones, I wondered, "How did the builder move these large pieces?" It certainly was back-breaking work, but even in this menial task, great pride was reflected in the construction. It is a marvel how this necessary work was even completed. Necessary, because these rock walls cordoned off pastures, fields, roadways, and boundaries. Our early settlers were certainly not afraid of hard work.

Slowly, my son and I continued to climb. The sun streamed down through the leaves as shadows danced on the green grass and roadbed. I could almost hear the previous owners of the area calling for us to continue enjoying what they had built.

Walking along, I began to contemplate whether the Bracketts were ever hungry. Did their children go to bed without food? How did the mountain get the name, Hunger? I will never know the answers to these questions unless I do some more research.

At any rate, we were coming to what appeared to be the first set of buildings. On both sides of the lane beyond the rock walls, old apple trees and grown up fields began to appear. Shortly, we approached an old house.

The entrance facing the lane was still standing, but the remainder of the building, shed, and outhouse had fallen down. The old, plaster walls and lathes had been crushed by the roof that had rotted away and fallen into the cellar hole. We climbed around the old rubble, digging here and there without success. In fact we explored all around the premises and found nothing.

Finally, we crossed the road where the barn had stood and explored that area. An old tote road could be seen leaving the barn area and following a gully away from the barn yard. In following this road for a short distance, my son came upon an old dump. It had been dug by a previous fellow bottle hound. However, we decided to scratch around anyway, and lo and behold we unearthed several bottles. In our digging we found many broken bottles. Pieces of one bottle indicated it had been an old soda. Scripture and Parker, 31 Court Square, Boston, was embossed in the green glass. Much to our amazement we found all the pieces to the bottle. As a note of interest, I glued the pieces together and this prize has become very valuable in our collection. It also answered one of the previous questions; if my great, great-grandfather's children had soda to drink, the chances are they were not lacking for food.

Returning to the old house, I walked out back where the outhouse had once stood. On the ground, covered with grass and other boards and debris, I found the old door to the outhouse. One of the old boards in the door had the year 1889 painted on it in red. This was indeed a treasure. This door, or rather a section of the board with the year painted on it, was made into a clock by my brother and to this day adorns my son's porch in his home—circa 1786.

Somewhat discouraged, we moved on across the top of the mountain to the two old ramshackled dwellings that were home to my great, great-uncles and their families. We found the dumps and a few old bottles at these locations, but once again they had previously been dug. The round trip back to the car was about four miles. We were tired, dirty, and smelling like Mother Earth, and on a more positive note we were filled with the memory of Hunger Mountain. Might I add, we were also very hungry.

Several times over the years we visited this mountain, and we still get a thrill walking over the ground once cultivated by our ancestors. As we ate our lunch that day, we realized another old road passed by the cemetery and disappeared into the forest. We took out an old map, and, sure enough, the roadway led to another set of buildings. This area was called Mantor Mountain. We proceeded up over a hill on a rutted tote road, and there we found the foundations. We looked around and hunted and hunted for an old dump without success. Returning to the car, we finally left this area of Starks and headed for home.

It has dawned on me that readers probably would like to know just where is this Kennebec River Valley? I am sure it would be helpful to familiarize yourself with this wilderness. The headwaters of the Kennebec begins north of Moosehead Lake and upper Somerset County. Seboomook Lake and Canada Falls Deadwater are tributaries to the Kennebec. Actually, the land divides on an east/west line, with waters north of these two bodies of water flowing east/west and providing the headwaters to the Penobscot River Valley. This eventually flows through Bangor, Maine and to the Atlantic Ocean through the Penobscot Bay. At the north end of Moosehead Lake to Merry Meeting Bay just north of Bath, Maine, the Kennebec flows south through Bath to the Atlantic. As the crow flies, this would be a trip of approximately 134 miles. Greenville, Maine, at the south end of Moosehead Lake, is considered the beginning of the river valley as it meanders south to Bath. This trip is considered by most people to be a 120 mile journey.

These 120 miles are where most of the towns in this book are located. Oh, we will stray east and west of the valley, but generally we will follow its course to the ocean. We will dig bottles from Greenville in the north, to Sidney and Augusta in the south and from Bangor, Maine in the east to Rangeley, Maine in the west.

To the interested reader, this area was of great significance to Maine's history. It was explored from the south to the north by primarily English settlers. They traveled the river to the interior and north to Canada. The French explored the north out of Quebec, Canada down the river south to the ocean.

It became obvious that sooner or later these different cultures would clash. This area is known for its Native American heritage and these Native American people were the catalyst that sparked much turmoil. This turmoil is documented in U.S. history, beginning with the French/Indian Wars through the American Revolution to Maine's statehood in 1820.

This book is not intended to trace the history of Maine. Others more qualified than I have done a great job outlining the significant historical timelines and exploration of this great state. Literary liberty has been taken, however, to point out that the governor of Massachusetts in great haste dispatched Captain Malton and several hundred men in 1724 to my hometown of Norridgewock in order to exterminate the Native American community founded by Father Sebastian Rales.

The remains of this massacre are etched in U.S. history books. Should the reader be unable to locate this terrible tragedy, the account has been inscribed on a granite stone on the original site at Father Sebastian Rales Monument. This area was the original village of the Norridgewock Indians. In later years (1775), when General Benedict Arnold traveled up the Kennebec with several other soldiers on his ill fated trip to Quebec Canada, Arnold noted in his diary the grave of Father Sebastian Rales was still visible. It is interesting to note a few Native American names associated with this section of the Kennebec. Bomazeen Rips, named after chief of the Norridgewock Tribe, and Oosoola and Skowhegan referring to sections of the Kennebec: "a place to watch" where Native Americans speared fish as they passed up or over some great falls just south of Norridgewock.

Previously, it was mentioned that bottle hunters should take along a first-aid kit on adventures into the wilderness. Safety is always a major concern, or at least it should be.. There are also things to watch out for that are almost always present and hidden from unsuspecting bottle hounds. Old wells are dangerous as most of the time if they are not covered safely. They can usually be located around the buildings a short distance from the kitchen or barn areas. Also, old, fallen down buildings usually have rusty nails protruding through the boards. Danger is everywhere in buildings reverting back to nature. Should you decide to scramble through the rubble, beams can fall, floors can give way, and walls can tumble down. Serious injury can be the result of being unaware of your surroundings.

I remember once running across a field and up a knoll and stumbling over an old well hole. Had I fallen in this hole, chances are I would, at the very least, have broken a bone. Also, bees' nests are very common in these old ruins, as are snakes, other nests, and burrows of many animals. The wise bottle hound is constantly aware of safety and uses his/her knowledge of the woods to their advantage. Protect yourself at all times!

Back home again and sometime later, my son, a friend, and I decided to go on another trip in Norridgewock. A dump had been located by my son. Every now and then the local power company (at that time it was known as Central Maine Power) would lower the water level by opening the dam at Skowhegan and closing the dam at Madison. This would have the effect of dropping the water level several feet in Norridgewock.

One day with the water level very low, my son climbed down over the bank of Mill Stream to cross over some mud flats. To his astonishment, he climbed down into an old dump and recognized several old bottles. This dump was off the west side of Oosoola Park beneath a huge, old pine tree.

To dig this dump, one would have to hang over the edge of the bank holding onto alders growing close by. Eventually a mound of dirt built up from digging and created a platform to stand on that helped in the process.

Mill Stream dumps into the Kennebec River just above the park. The stream got its name from an old grist mill that stood on the bank at the corner of what is now the intersection of Route 2, Route 8, and Route 139. Across the road from the mill an old mill house stood. This will be another adventure at a later time.

Returning to the park, the name Oosoola means pale or yellow flower. I think at one time this park was an interval farmed by families living along the short road leading into the park off Route 2. As I remember, there were three or four old homes along this road, one of which was occupied by a family of several children. In the mid-1970's two or three of the children somehow fell into the stream behind their home. The father heard the commotion and jumped into the water to save his children. The father could not swim, and all of the children and the father drowned.

Shortly after this tragedy, the town tore down the buildings and somehow Scott Paper Company became the owner of this interval. I think sometime later in the 1970's Scott Paper Company gave the property back to the town of Norridgewock to be used as a park. A sign has been erected beside the entrance to indicate this gift. Each year the town celebrates a frog jumping contest and other activities enjoyed by all. There is a boat landing, a children's playground, barbecue pits, and a gazebo used for musical concerts. I often wondered why the park was not called York Park to commemorate a father who could not swim jumping into the stream to save his children.

Now, my son had brought home several old beer bottles and other treasures, and he indicated the dump had hardly been touched. He returned again and again and never came home empty-handed. So, this particular day, we took our tools and walked several 100 yards to this site. My home is on a hill known as Waterville Hill, which is a short distance from the park.

We dug most of the day and found old whiskeys, medicinal bottles and an assortment of other valuable glass containers. The old pine tree was in our way, so we began to dig under and around its root system. Eventually, the entire root system was exposed, exposed so profoundly that you could crawl right under this stately old pine.

As we spent the afternoon talking, exchanging stories, and in general just plain enjoying ourselves an incident happened. Our friend who had accompanied us was on his back, tucked way up under the tree when he struck glass with his digger. There was no way the bottle would come loose, so he called for a saw to cut the root that was holding the bottle.

My son ran home, got a small, camp bow-saw and returned in a matter of minutes. The saw was passed to our friend, and he began the laborious job of sawing a large root off while he lay on his back struggling to stay in place. I remember we were somewhat uneasy that the tree might settle onto our friend, but he kept on sawing. His safety became a real concern. If the tree settled, I'm sure it would have been a terrible accident. He kept on sawing.

Finally, we heard him comment the bottle was loose and out of the hole he scrambled. He was holding a Warner's Safe Cure For Kidney and Liver and Brights' Disease bottle—the exact replica of the bottle I had found several years earlier behind the old door frame in my rumpus room. Yes, the same bottle that had started me on the search for old dumps. As each of us excitedly handled the bottle and passed it back and forth to admire, we noticed a flaw in the bottle. In looking closer, it became obvious that our friend had sawed into the bottle. The saw mark was of considerable depth but the bottle did not crack. What a memory! To this day that bottle is a joy to look at and recount the day it was found.

The old mill house provided another dump located on a steep bank opposite Oosoola Park. It was found when my son and some of his friends ran down the bank to escape from whatever boys will run from. As they reached the bottom of the hill, glass tumbled down onto the pavement making a clinking noise. The boys ran back up the hill and began scratching behind the old house. Sure enough, bottles began to surface.

The next day, we both walked back to the spot. Twenty or thirty bottles were found. I remember digging under an old apple tree stump and locating several bottles that were added to my collection. On two or three occasions, we returned to the site and came home rewarded for our efforts. One bottle in particular stands out in my mind from this dump. It was an old, pottery ink well that now sits on the mantle over the fireplace in my home.

While considering this area, it reminds me of other dumps found on the banks of the Kennebec River: Dumps that provided Hostetter's Bitters, beautiful old cruets, several different ink bottle types from cone to umbrella, medicinal and household bottles, canning jars, spice bottles, and flavoring extract bottles. These bottles' styles ranged from high and low ball neck bottles, flared lips, applied lips, blob tops, and crown tops. Most of these make up a sizable portion of my collection. We made a great find along the river when we found three generations of the old Moxie Nerve Food bottle—an applied lip, blob top, and crown top. These bottles preceded the Moxie soda sold today in Maine stores. Each year the town of Lisbon, Maine holds a celebration to honor the creator of this drink.

Many times I have put my 12 foot aluminum boat in the river at the Oosoola Boat Landing and taken leisurely trips up and down this wondrous ribbon of water, looking for dumps or just fishing for brown trout at Bomazeen Rips. As I motor along, I often wonder what the bottom of the river would hold for treasures.

Once, when the Central Maine Power Company lowered the river, Nathan and I walked along the muddy slope and found several bottles. One was deep down the muddy slope almost in the channel, left by the receding water. It was a small, green bottle with "Lamping-Noland, Boston's own" embossed in the glass. If we found this stuck in the mud deep down in the channel, I'm sure there are many others that were either thrown in the river or washed down it over the years by the spring freshets. Someone with scuba diving equipment could probably locate a wealth of antique bottles in the river. My brother used to put on scuba diving demonstrations for sportsman shows. Someday I guess I'll give him a call and ask his opinion and possible help.

The river holds many secrets and casts a spell over the interested adventurer. Gliding along in boat, you will see the overgrown black growth of spruce, fir, hemlock and pine give way to oak, birch, poplar and maple. Now and then brooks and streams can be heard rippling over rocks as the water empties in the Kennebec. Further north near the town of Madison, the Sandy River dumps into the Kennebec. This spot is just south of the old Norridgewock Native American village that was destroyed by Captain Malton in 1724. It has been written that the women, children and old people of the village tried desperately to flee from this massacre by running into the river. They could not escape and were killed at random.

Sitting on a river in a boat bobbing along has a tendency to place you in a trance. In this blissful state of mind, I often think of how much the river meant to my ancestors. It was used in almost all aspects of survival. The fact that the river provided easy traveling over the many miles from the great Moosehead Lake to the Atlantic Ocean was just minor convenience compared to the river feeding and providing for populations of people settling along its banks. It provided ice to preserve food in the hot months of summer, fish to sustain a variety of animals including human beings, water for the settlers in the awakening wilderness to quench their thirst or to wash or bathe, or just plain recreation.

In days past, the river was used for log drives, to run mills, and even today for hydro-electric power. The river was generally clear and clean during the era of exploration and was primarily used for transportation. During the awakening of the wilderness by lumberjacks and log drives, the river became polluted. Especially with the advent of early paper mills, the toxic chemicals were either accidentally spilled or dumped into the river. This killed the fish and created a cesspool of filth and stench.

How the Native Americans must have hated this American Industrial Revolution. Thank the good Lord that our politicians saw fit to change this terrible direction we were flowing in. In 1976, our country's Bicentennial birthday, the last log drive was held, and the water in the river has continuously improved since. Today we can not only swim in the river, but also we can eat the fish and drink the water again. This improvement continued with the Clean Water Act, thus eliminating raw sewage from being dumped directly into the river. Each town along the confluence of the river has put in sewer treatment plants, and individual rural homes and farms built their own sewer systems far removed from the natural waterway.

Up and down the Kennebec River, I have spotted old dumps from past generations using its banks to hide their trash. One of the first town dumps in Norridgewock was off Depot Street over a bank leading down into the Mill Stream. This dump was probably used throughout the 18th and 19th century. In the 20th century, the town dump was located north of the village off the Winding Hill Road. Again, this dump was located very close to the river.

Each of these dumps helped to pollute the river. I'm sure most communities from Greenville to Bath along the river were guilty of this trash hiding technique. Each of these dumps in Norridgewock has given up bottle treasures to this hound and other hounds. I have hundreds of bottles an antique dealer would grab without batting an eye. Some of these prizes found in these dumps were historical flasks (a few), pepper sauce bottles including cathedral pickles, many bottles with pontil marks, whiskey flasks, and ruby red beer bottles. These are just a few of the treasures.

In this century town dumps are carefully monitored to ensure surrounding areas are not polluted. The old dumps in Norridgewock and other communities are slowly disappearing. Many have been capped, and the environment has hidden the remainder.

A brief description of the town of Norridewock might enlighten readers as to what other towns along the banks of the mighty Kennebec River are like. For example, during the early years of exploration, towns in general were surveyed off in six mile squares or 36 square miles in area. Sections of the town were designated tax free for religious purposes and land was provided for schools. Norridgewock was incorporated as a town in 1788 as were the towns of Winslow and Fairfield just south of Norridgewock. Other towns to the north, west and east of Norridgewock were incorporated in later years. Towns to the south generally were incorporated earlier than Norridgewock.

As a rule, the further north you travel from the Atlantic Ocean, the later the towns were organized. Some of the towns in Southern Maine were incorporated in the early 18th century. Populations in these towns vary; however, in Norridgewock the population has remained stable for decades. The population today is approximately 2,500 people. A quick check of square miles times population provides a density in Norridgewock of 60 people per square mile. This is relatively sparse compared to that of Portland, Maine with a density of approximately 90 per square mile.

As for the population density of the state, it's approximately 30 people per square mile.

These two descriptions of area and population density raise some interesting points to ponder. Is there still wilderness in Maine to be explored? If so, could one find adventures in this wilderness? With towns being incorporated from the early 18th century, would this wilderness hide yesteryear's old dumps? The answer is yes to both questions. There are many adventures to be enjoyed in Maine and treasures to be found. All it takes is a desire to explore what is in your backyard.

In this age of technology, people tend to forget the fun and enjoyment of just walking through the forest. They seem to have forgotten how to use their senses to smell the rain, see the eagle, touch a dew drop, taste the wild berries of the forest, or drink from an old spring bubbling out of the forest floor. Yes, many have forgotten how it feels to walk on green moss, or wade shoeless through a mountain stream. Such skills as identifying the types of trees in the forest, the birds in the sky, or the animals in the forest seem to have disappeared.

I'll never understand how someone can ignore these wonderful opportunities that await us in nature. These opportunities instill a wealth of knowledge and experience in us that is far superior to the material wealth of the present day society. So, move away from your personal computer, VCR, T.V., and all the other high tech gadgets you own and come with me to the unexplored regions of your backyard. Place these marvelous technological things in perspective as they are important in today's world, but balance this world of technology with the free gifts the creator has provided for each of us.

Off we go on another adventure! This time we're going to Freeman, Maine. This is a town located west of Norridgewock about 35 miles and is closer to the northern extension of the White Mountains. As my whole family is going as well as dear friends, we are taking two vehicles. We travel to Farmington and on to Philips across an old bridge and enter the domain of dirt roads. Our destination is a mountain introduced to me as Richards' Mountain. It seems my father was born in this area. I'm returning to locate the old homestead foundation.

We brought along old county maps and my trusty *Maine Atlas,* as well as the *Gazetteer* to help in locating Richards' Mountain. Scouting around, we came across a farmer leading his work horse down the road. Stopping the cars, I got out to talk to the apparent owner of the horse. As I approached the rear of the horse, it was only natural to place my hand on the horse's rump to rest one leg as I asked the farmer for directions. Quite a while passed, as he studied our maps. Finally, he uttered some directions. When I asked, "Where does the road go?" He answered, "This road doesn't go anywhere, it stays right here." I chuckled as I returned to the car.

The greatest joke was still to come. Sitting in the cars, everyone had noticed how I had leaned on the rump of the horse since they were behind the horse and my back was turned, it was only natural to compare my posture to that of the horse's tush. I'm sure I did look silly leaning on that horse's rump. To this day, my family still laughs at that rear-end picture.

We traveled down the road, following the farmer's directions. A few miles later, we came to the spot we were trying to locate. Parking the cars, we took our diggers, picnic lunch, and excited talk over to the opening in the forest where an old tote road led up a long hill and disappeared in the distance. There were seven of us including my wife. We began to climb and climb and climb, and an hour later we were still climbing.

This roadbed had been used by horse and buggy or wagon. Where the wagon wheels dug into the dirt on either side of the road, over time the dirt had washed away. The road was at such a steep pitch that we had to work at maintaining our balance. In the middle of the two washed-away wheel tracks, the soil was raised and grass grew in this section. This became the path that we followed. Several miles later we arrived at an old cellar hole or foundation. It was located beside the road, and from the size of the hole, it must have been a huge homestead.

Looking back down the mountain, it became apparent why the home was built in this location. The forest opened wide to the sky, and you could look for miles over the dense wilderness. Not a man-made structure was in view. Once again, in reflecting on the homesteaders that lived here, I could only marvel at their adventuresome spirit and strength of character.

All seven of us studied the landscape and worked the theories of locating where the dump may have been. We found nothing, but enjoyed the peacefulness and serenity of this mountain top as we ate our picnic. I sat on one of the old granite blocks used for the foundation, and something caught my eye inside the cellar hole. Jumping into the hole that had trees 8" to 10" in diameter growing up through the ground, I reached down underneath some old bricks—remains of the chimney— and I pulled from the mud a beautiful crystal, bar whiskey bottle, clear in color with sunbursts in the glass.

Did I feel great? You bet, and I let everyone know just how great I did feel. This bottle was to be protected at all costs as it was found in the house my father was born in back in the year 1906. The seam stopped at the shoulder, indicating the bottle could probably be dated to the middle to late 1800's. My grandfather Richards may have sat in the coolness of his cellar high up on that mountain drinking the contents of that bottle while my grandmother was delivering my father upstairs. At any rate, it was a valuable find for my growing collection.

It was beginning to get late, and we all turned our attention back down the mountain. All of the sudden my wife began to show great stress. It seems she had taken the keys from the car's ignition and placed them in her pocket. Somewhere along the trail or road bed she had lost them. They were nowhere to be found.

With fallen spirits, we began to descend the mountain. As we walked along, we tried to keep each other comforted. At no time was blame placed on my wife. The talk was more about who would be left behind as some of the tired troop went for help. It was even proposed that, since I had liked the horse so much earlier, I might enjoy riding him back to town. We continued to walk in the middle of the road bed where the grass was growing as we had walked on the ascent.

Excitement suddenly broke forth from the front of the line. One of the children had actually found the keys in the pathway. We all hooted and hollered, and our spirits simply soared. Our trip up the mountain had not only tested our stamina, but also our honest concern for each other's feelings. Once again, this experience had brought us closer together as a family. It also left a lasting memory with our friends which has never been forgotten. Imagine finding those keys! I'm convinced there is a master plan imposed on each of us by a Greater Being. If you're in the right place at the right time and your heart is pure, only goodness can prevail.

Looking up the road from where we were parked, we spotted an old house with a falling down garage beside the road. The foundation under the house was caving in, but it did look like someone had lived there off and on through the year. Looking in the garage, we saw a very early Ford Coupe in pretty good condition. It was a shame to see it being exposed to the elements.

We tried to find out who owned the building, as we wanted to ask if we could buy this prize. We were not successful. In later years, I returned and the old car was gone. Might I also add, several more trips were made to the town of Freeman with success. Many bottles were bought back from other old 19th century dumps. Traveling home we were very tired, dirty, thirsty, lame, and just plain worn out.

This same motley crew of bottle hounds went on another trip to the town of Farmington. The site was very close to the town line of Starks. In fact, somewhere back in the woods we crossed over its west boundary. We had found the old discontinued country road from old maps of the area. It was in the spring of the year just after black fly season. Our adventure started by an old cemetery and dipped down a steep hill. It was a beautiful day and we were all feeling energetic and excited.

As we followed the old road down the hill we could hear the bubbling of a brook or stream. The water was cascading over rocks and making sounds that are very familiar to a brook fisherman. Coming closer, we found ourselves walking over a very old earthen and field rock bridge. I'm sure it had been constructed back in the early 19th century. Later on I found out we had walked across a treasured Maine landmark called Thompson's Bridge. It was a wonderful example of Maine ingenuity, constructed wholly out of field stones and placed meticulously to form a bridge about 30' long and 10' or 12' high. Dirt was hauled in over the rocks and built up to the level of the roadbed. I walked down over the edge of the roadbed to the huge pool of water below the bridge and sat on a stone. Looking back at the bridge there was a square opening the width of the road bed with the water crossing through like a huge culvert. This was indeed a treasure that was enjoyed by each of us as we studied its colonial architectural design. I had no idea this bridge would cross over to a path that led even further into the bowels of the forest.

Moving on, we spotted some huge tell-tale maple trees that lined the entrance to several foundations. We scoured around and eventually found ourselves on a granite slope behind what appeared to be the old house. It could have been the shed or barn, we just couldn't tell. The slope slid off toward the stream.

In looking up or down the stream, embedded in the water were great boulders. I could also see huge potholes. My geology experience told me these holes were made in the granite when a smaller rock got caught in a swirling eddy. Over time, as the rock swirled and twirled, it carved out the hole, with rock grinding against rock.

Looking back up the slope, we began to dig beneath alders, old bushes, field grass, burdocks, and some small trees. We found a few bottles, but nothing too exciting. We explored further up the road and found another old fallen down building. There was a rock wall behind the house, and in that rock wall and on the backside of it we struck pay dirt. Several very valuable bottles were found as we actually rearranged the wall.

It was getting along toward one o'clock and hunger pangs were rumbling in our stomachs, so we decided to go back to the bridge and eat our picnic. It was one of those days that makes you feel glad you're alive! Days that are filled with joy as your senses are very acute and you're in tune not only with yourself, but with your surroundings. We enjoyed the afternoon in the woods, later studying the old grave stones at the cemetery we had passed on our way into Thompson's Bridge.

Years ago when there were no fences, these early settlers cleared the land by digging out rocks from their fields, and they used those rocks to build rock walls. These walls were and are really works of art. Many times they would build walls over the household dump to protect their animals from being cut from broken glass.

In the field, I can just see an old-timer using Archimedes Principle of the Level to pry a huge boulder out of the ground. Next, he probably wrapped a chain around it and hooked it to his team of horse or oxen. They, in turn, pulled it over to what was going to be the boundary of his field. The smaller rocks were tiered up several feet high in two parallel walls. These walls were carefully constructed and piled neatly about three feet apart. Next, smaller rocks picked from the fields were thrown in-between these parallel walls to fill in the crevice. Each year as the frost pushed rocks nearer the surface and the old-timer plowed his fields, these rocks would have to be picked up and hauled to and placed in the growing rock wall.

As I observe some of these walls, this is how I think they were built. The walls are numerous all through Maine and New England. They are found far removed from today's hustle and bustle of communities. Now and then you can see one as you drive the highways and byways of the country. Usually, the best examples are found way back in what was once cultivated land that has now reverted back to nature. Have you ever stopped to look at one of these walls? Just think of the tremendous amount of work it took to section off fields, fence in animals, or create a boundary line. Today, I cringe at the thought of having to work beside these old-timers.

While I'm on the subject of old walls or boundary lines, split-rails were also used for the same purpose. They were known as "split rail fences." Usually, the rails were split from cedar trees. A cedar would be cut down, cut into 10', 12' or 16' sections. These sections were then split into quarters. Finally, they were either placed on top of rock walls or placed free standing with posts driven into the ground at either end of a rail. I have seen rail fences from 3 to 6 rails tall.

Another treasure that is around my home in Norridgewock is a split rail fence. Many years ago, the rails were hauled by hand out of the backwoods by my son and me. They were found on the old farm owned by my step-grandfather and grandmother. The farm was originally owned by my step-grandfather's father. This places the farm back in the early 19th century. The rails were made out of cedar and are as solid today as they were 150 years ago. I have taken a knife and whittled away some of the old silver, weathered, outer wood, and the inside is clear and dry, still giving off that glorious cedar odor. There are thirteen 16' sections of fence facing the main road in front of my home and twenty-one 16' sections surrounding my in-ground swimming pool out behind the barn. Might I add, across the road my son has since found old rails and framed his home with this same kind of fence. They are great fences for framing our old colonial homes, and they look very picturesque and blend well with the old community of Norridgewock, Maine.

This next excursion is to explore an old ghost town in Maine. Actually, it is listed as a ghost town. Its name is Bowerbank, and it is about 55 miles north of Norridgewock, about 10 miles northeast of the town of Milo. Years ago, my wife's grandparents were local merchants in Norridgewock and had many friends. For their enjoyment, these folks would travel to an old homestead in Bowerbank. They called themselves the Eagles. They played cards and did whatever else their generation did for fun. I was told the ladies baked biscuits and pies and competed as to who was the best cook. Beans were baked, and I can imagine the men folk had a tighter belt when they returned to their hometown.

The trip to locate this homestead was uneventful. Oh, we enjoyed the trip, but we were anxious to get started on the real purpose of our journey, to find old bottles. After a couple of hours, we arrived at Bowerbank and found the old homestead.

The Eagle's Nest, as it was affectionately called by the Eagles, was an old, early 19th century dwelling. It had the same architectural design as mentioned before—big house, little house, back-house, barn—with another large barn downwind from the house. The main house was painted an off-white with purple trim and had wooden shutters covering the windows. A large porch surrounded the front of the house with granite steps leading into it. Directly in front of the granite steps was a large, old, iron pump that still worked. The house and surroundings reminded me of something someone from the Walton's T.V. program would call home. The lawns had all gone back to nature, but you could see where the garden plot was located. The old place had not been lived in for years.

We spread out blankets on the lawn and began to eat our picnic. As we ate, we sized up the old place. Each of us looked for a spot to explore. After lunch, my friend's wife had to go "visit nature." Returning from across the road a few minutes later, she was holding several bottles in her hands. She unknowingly asked, "Are these any good?" We couldn't believe what she had brought back. A Mexican Mustang Liniment, John Wyeth & Bro., canning jars, Florida Water, Hock Wine, a pepper sauce, and a couple of old Sarsaparilla bottles. Obviously, we asked her where nature had called. When we reached the place, we found a few more bottles strewn over the forest floor. Since then and on other trips, we would always ask her if "nature is calling."

We dug in other places at the Eagles' Nest without success, and finally we walked several hundred yards down an old road further back in the woods. As we rounded a bend, we came upon what appeared to be a logical place to dig. Besides, my nose was telling me something was close by. I remember pushing over an old, rotten stump and finding a few 44-40 rifle shells. They still had lead in the end of the casing. Years ago a hunter may have emptied his rifle while leaning against the tree or got buck fever as he spotted a deer or bear and emptied his rifle on the ground. At any rate, it was a different find.

Close by, there were the remnants of an old dump. We found some more treasures and continued to scout around the old building. In a swale hole behind the house cordoned off by a rock wall, we began to dig more bottles, and we even found relics like clothes' irons, pots and pans, and horse harness bells. These iron relics still adorn my rumpus room. Over the years, I have found many old brass bells, door knockers, and foot scrapers. Once a long time ago, my son walked out of the woods with a large piece of granite with a beautiful foot scraper still in tact. This foot scraper was placed at the entrance to his home and is still used to this day.

Coming back to the task at hand, we had pretty much dug out the swale hole and had walked out to the old road to get our bearings. We looked around and one of the children was missing. The child was about ten years old, and since we called and called with no answer, we assumed the worst. Some of us panicked as the Maine woods can be frightening if you are in an area that is unfamiliar. We hollered, shouted, ran back and forth, and up and down the road to no avail. This went on for a couple of hours. We were very concerned.

After we had pretty much worn ourselves out with worry, we looked up the road, and down the road came our lost offspring. Seems our lost child was never worried and knew exactly where we were at all times. The hood on the child's coat was pulled over her head, so she couldn't hear us calling her name. Yes, she was scolded and told to stay close for the rest of the day. Years later, this same child was seen laying in the middle of an old tote road, hood up, face down, trying to escape the dreaded Maine black flies and mosquitoes. We headed home full of fresh visions of the Maine woods and chucker block-full of stories and excitement.

Maine winters can be fierce. Not only cold, but deep snow and ice that can make the traveling dangerous. I have often wondered, how many of these old bottles could possibly survive a winter. Especially for over one hundred years buried out in the wilderness close to the surface. The Maine winters drive the frost deep into the ground surrounding these bottles. Being an old die-hard bottle digger, I have actually dug bottles in late fall with frost in the ground. There have been times I would find a bottle and note where it was so I could come back in the spring to dislodge it.

Talking about winter reminds me of how I started the collecting of old electric insulators. Years ago my son, a friend, and I became aware of the old railroad bed running north and south through Norridgewock. telephone poles lined the old bed for miles. On the poles that were left standing were old glass insulators.

One winter day, we decided to find some way to salvage them before they were lost or broken by hunters. We called an old, retired friend who used to be a line-man for Central Maine Power Company. We asked if we could use his pole climbers. He said yes, and before we knew it, we were off on another adventure.

We walked for miles along an old non-used railroad bed. Each pole that had insulators on the cross pieces was climbed. We collected many shapes and sizes and brought them home. The snow depth that year was much greater than this year, 1999. As I recall, we waded in snow way above our knees and were cold and wet upon returning home. This year in the middle of January, we have no snow on the grounds.

When I was a boy back in the 1940's we experienced a far greater amount of snow. In 1951, we had such a blizzard no one could travel for days. So, somewhere between that blizzard of '51 and this year's (1999) lies a typical Maine winter. Usually, the cold is what keeps us inside. The temperature can range from 40 degrees below zero to 50 degrees above in the coldest months—December through February. In other places in Maine, the winters can be even more severe.

Those insulators were displayed in my rumpus room until one day something happened. My neighbor had given me an old canning jar made out of flint glass. It was a wide mouth quart jar and being flint glass, if you snapped it with your finger, it would resonate like cut crystal. One day, I was doing something foolish by handling an old insulator directly over this prize canning jar. I dropped the insulator, and it struck the jar shattering it into a million pieces. Without hesitation all the insulators were retired to the barn where they remain to this day.

Talking about my neighbor brings me to her beautiful old colonial home that used to be a hospital. The date it was built, 1811, is chiseled into the granite step leading into the house. The home/hospital is considered to be older, though, more like circa 1803. If you know your history, 1803 should tell you of the Louisiana Purchase, the Lewis and Clark Expedition, and of Thomas Jefferson being President.

The old hospital had an original backhouse on the second floor, just off the operating room. Yes, I asked my neighbor if I could dig around under the old three-holer. She agreed, and I crawled under the old shed and began to dig around. Sure enough, I began to find all kinds of valuable bottles: whiskies, medicinal, household, inks, beer, flasks, and old soda bottles were just some of the finds. I came away with several bushel baskets full of bottles.

I remember giving my neighbor a basket full, and I have often wondered what happened to them as she wasn't into the hobby of digging old bottles. On her mantel over an old granite fireplace, she had an old Fairbanks Beard soda bottle. One fall, my son raked the leaves on her whole lawn which was a considerable area, for that bottle. That Christmas my son gave me that bottle as a present. It now sits on my mantel as a conversation piece, and people remark on its beautiful, teal green color. At a later time, my neighbor allowed me to use a metal detector to scour her lawn for other treasures. I can't recall any bottles, but do remember digging her lawn up like my Swiss cheese lawn years earlier. We did eventually fill in the holes and had a great time sharing our hobby with her.

This hobby has some very tedious cleaning attached to finalizing a bottle for display. Bottles brought home after being buried for years in the ground are stained with residue and need careful attention. An unclean bottle is very objectionable. So time, patience, determination, and perseverance are necessary to bring a bottle to its beauty.

Tools necessary for this procedure are varied. I have used everything from small bits of gravel to sections of coat hangers. Actually, anything that works to clean off residue or stains is acceptable. Care must be used not to scratch the bottle or crack the glass.

Some helpful hints to protect a bottle that I have learned from experience are:

1. If the bottle has been brought in from cold weather, let the bottle adjust to room temperature. Too often, I have washed a bottle in warm or hot water and later on heard the ear splitting "clink" as a real prize bottle has cracked from the expansion and contraction of the glass.

2. In using B B's or small pieces of gravel, be very careful in shaking the bottle as its shoulders are very thin and can easily break or crack.

3. To clean out hardened material in the bottom of a bottle, coat hangers are very useful. Bend the tip of a coat hanger over to alleviate scratching of the inside of the bottle.

4. Do not let small children handle your prize treasures. Too often they do not know the value of the bottle. My most prized bottles are displayed in a curio cabinet or some other cabinet with a door that can be locked.

Other hints in cleaning bottles are to fill them with a detergent. Vinegar is helpful. Let a bottle with a stubborn stain soak in a solution for a few days. I have used everything from Comet to gasoline. A word of caution: *do not mix your chemicals.* Always be aware of safety and especially of possible chemical reactions. Some bottles have been stained from acids or minerals in the ground. This is sometimes called "sick glass," and it may never be able to be cleaned. For display purposes, collectors have been known to cover their bottles with a light coating of oil for a short time. This covers up many imperfections. A word to the wise: if you are in an antique shop always be leery of bottles that appear very slick or shiny.

Obviously, with hundreds of bottles, cleaning them can be an awesome chore. Usually my treasures from an adventure are placed on shelves in my barn. These considerable shelves have and still are filled with bottles. Every now and then, I spend a day, or even a few days, doing nothing but cleaning. My son has boxes of wonderful old antique bottles out in his barn that are still not cleaned. When one has thousands of bottles, cleaning becomes a chore.

The next adventure was a close call with my life. It taught me something about never going bottle digging alone. It all began on a trip to Hampshire Hill in the town of Mercer just a few miles west of Norridgewock.

In the month of May, my son and I started out to where our old maps reflected a long deserted community that once was prosperous. It was up on top of a hill that seemed more like a mountain, way back off a dirt road long since reverted back to nature. Once again we passed an old, long forgotten cemetery dating back to the early 1800's. As we walked along, patches of snow still clung to the roadside and in the woods. This was also the beginning of mud season and streams of water were running down the ditches.

As we started to climb the hill, gullies were washed out in the roadway, and brooks were literally tumbling down over the rocks. The running water was music to our ears as it danced over rocks and spilled over small waterfalls. The forest was clear of leaves as new buds were just beginning to show on the limbs of the hardwoods.

It was peaceful and serene as we walked along ever upward. Without the leaves, you could look back and observe the mountains in the distance. Every now and then I could hear the call of a crow or blue jay warning the forest creatures of our intrusion. You could see for miles!

Walking along, I began to feel what I thought was indigestion: That burning sensation I used to call heartburn or acidic stomach. Over the years this sensation has been part of my daily living. This time, however, the feeling kept getting worse. It was so bad, in fact, that I would have to stop for it to dissipate.

Finally, desperate people do desperate things. I was cupping my hands, scooping water out of the ditch to drink, but I couldn't get enough water. Looking around, I found an old beer can tossed up into the woods by some thoughtless hunter or woodsman. This can I rinsed out, filled with water, and as I walked I would drink. Even with this pacifier, every 100 yards or so I would have to stop until the pain would subside. My son probably thought we would never get to where we were going.

This procedure continued all the way up the hill. It appeared that, the more I exercised, the more frequently the pain came. I kept telling my son, "Boy this is a real good case of indigestion, the worst I ever experienced." Arriving at the crest of the hill, the forest and the old road bed leveled out. Walking became easier; I could now walk a couple of hundred yards without stopping.

After what felt like ten miles we came to the old foundations that we were looking for. Old apple trees were everywhere. At one time, this must have been an orchard where people came to buy apples. There were too many trees for just one family to use. We scouted around and found a gully where, over the years, rocks had been dumped. Broken, old, glass bottles were strewn over and between the rocks.

As I still wasn't feeling too energetic, my son began moving rocks. You guessed it! What to our wondering eyes did appear, but old bottles. Even though my indigestion was still bothering me, I pitched right in with the search. This was one time my excitement could have killed me. Every so often, I would have to stop, drink from the old beer can, and complain to anyone listening how the pain was killing me.

We found several old inks and many household bottles. After awhile, I said to my son, "I'm going to start down over the hill." I thought he could stay longer, as I was slowed by my constant stopping to alleviate the chest pain. Still feeling great discomfort, I began to head back to the car. Later, I found out the round trip was only about four miles.

On the way out I came to a fork in the old road. Sitting down, I waited for my son. Shortly he came along. We looked at the map and sure enough, the left road led to a couple of other old foundations. I was feeling good enough by then to go to the left. We walked a short distance through some snow, and on the right side of the road we saw the remains of yet another old, fallen-down structure.

Snow covered most everything, but we were able to break through the frost in several places. We found some old metal treasures, broken glass, many old hand-hewn beams and silver hemlock boards, but no bottles. Digging in the snow was very frustrating. Not only did your hands get cold, but we became very wet and uncomfortable. Being the forever optimist, I declared, "At least there were no pesky black flies or mosquitoes."

It was getting late, and we began the descent out of the woods and down over the mountain. I was still experiencing discomfort and walked slowly. My son stayed close in front of me as I slipped and slid down the hill. Finally, we reached the car.

This was the first and only time I was extremely pleased to be out of the woods and on the way home. Just sitting in the car without activity seemed to make me feel better. Sure, I was bloated from all the water and had to stop every so often to satisfy the call of nature. Thankfully, we arrived home, and I took to my easy chair in front of the television.

Around 7:00 p.m., I began to have great discomfort with indigestion. My concern was heightened because I hadn't eaten anything. The pain got worse and worse, so finally I made the decision to go to the emergency room at our local hospital. Having never had heart trouble before, I was shocked when the doctor said, "I think you're either having a heart attack or a severe case of angina." My blood pressure was sky high and by this time the pain was continuous.

To make this long story short, I was sent to the Eastern Maine Medical Center at Bangor, Maine where the doctors found I had three arteries that were plugged. After they inserted three stints in the arteries, I was sent home. Several months would pass before I would venture back into the Maine woods. The lessons from this adventure to Hampshire Hill was twofold: think twice before going alone on long trips in the Maine woods, and if something in your body doesn't feel right, don't take it for granted, go see a doctor. My indigestion was a close call with a heart attack! As you might imagine, this trip slowed this old fellow down considerably. I did use the time wisely. I cleaned hundreds of old bottles. I am now going on other adventures, but I dig at a slower pace. My enjoyment has been elevated to a higher level since realizing these adventures can't go on indefinitely.

Thinking back about the time I have lived in Norridgewock, several old-timers come to mind. One was a trapper living in a small, two-room shack on the outskirts of town. He also loved to hunt bobcats with his two Blue tick hounds. I visited him in my younger years on several occasions. I was always welcome and would pull up a chair in front of his old wood stove and listen to his stories. He loved house cats and they were everywhere in the shack. They were well fed, as were his hounds. This old hermit chewed tobacco, and as he talked he would spit at any opening on the stove. It appeared as though he missed more than he hit. I am sure he hadn't changed clothes, taken a bath, or cleaned his palace for many a moon. The stench could be overwhelming, but it was his house.

As I was a visitor, I always showed him respect and was polite. He usually had several skins of varying kinds hanging inside on the wall. These skins were his livelihood. As we talked he would sit in front of his old stove, scraping the tallow from a skin he had just skinned off one of his trapped animals. This old fellow was almost always in the woods either hunting or trapping.

As he related to me, he often came across old dumps far removed from present day villages, towns, or neighborhoods. He had the bottles to prove it. I never saw such a collection of old bitters bottles and historical flasks in my life. He actually was wealthy. Some of his bottles were valued at hundreds of dollars! Now that he has passed away, I have often wondered what happened to his collection.

He taught me much about my town. I got great joy listening to him tell about his Blue tick hounds. He would take them out after a new-fallen snow, let them loose on a track, and follow their yodeling for miles. This usually took him around and around for hours. Cats would take to the mountains when they knew dogs where on their trail. He often spoke of startling a bobcat on Doddlin Mountain to the west of town, tracking it down through Canada Meadows, to Bear Mountain in the south, and then across Martin Stream to Green Mountain in the southwest. "Those cats sure tuckered me out" he would say. In his travels, he came across many old dumps and shared their location with me. To this day I'm forever grateful.

The other old timer lived with his mother. He was a bachelor and a woodsman. Many an old maid felt he would be a good catch, but he managed to stay one step ahead of them. He was one strong Frenchman and spoke with a strong accent. Most woodsmen in town respected his knowledge of the woods to know how to make a good living and he worked harder than most men. He was a kind man and would share most anything. Some would say he was "woods queer" from spending so much time alone. I have come across him in the woods cooking his meal while standing in front of a roaring fire built out of evergreen branches. Might I add, he always smelled of evergreen smoke as this was his world. Now, he too is also dead. I'm glad I got to know this character; it was an education. He shared many a location where I have since found bottles.

These two old-timers were the last remnants in our town of strong character built on a deep commitment and knowledge of the Maine woods. They respected the environment and took no more from it than what they needed to survive. I'll miss them in these days of environmental unthoughtfulness. Just look around at today's clearcutting and the abuse of those giant paper companies. The paper companies talk the talk, but don't walk the walk!

If the reader is wondering are we always welcome on others property to dig for old bottles, the answer is, "No!" I remembered a trip to Tarbel Hill with my son and my father-in-law. We had found the area we wanted to explore, found no bottles, and were on the way across the field heading to the car. All of a sudden, we heard the saltiest language directed at us. "What are you b.a.s.t.a.r.d.s. doing? Who the h.e.l.l. gave you permission to go on that property? Get the h.e.l.l. out of here before I call the cops!"

Coming close to the car, we could see an old woman outside her home a couple of hundred yards down the road. She was really pealing us out. Well, my father-in-law stood it for a few minutes and then began to fire back some of his own salty language. The air was blue with these two firing verbal abuses back and forth.

In driving off, my father-in-law said, "Stop at that house!" So I stopped. Much to my amazement, these two people knew each other. Coming eyeball to eyeball, I soon learned that this old woman and my father-in-law had been friends for years. They reminisced for a long time and left each other as friends. She told us, "Come on back, ya hear!"

On another occasion, my son and some of his friends were digging at the old Norridgewock town dump off Depot Street. They returned with many bottles. Later that evening, I received a telephone call from the son of the woman living just up near the bank where the dump was located. His comments were far from polite. His main concern was the banking of his mother's lawn, which had been disturbed because the boys had dug a trench just over the edge.

He lit into me, making it quite clear that I was to come down to his mother's place and fill in the trench.

Not knowing what he was talking about, I fired back with a little salty language of my own. The conversation ended with him informing me he was going to call the sheriff. Sure enough, the sheriff came to my home after receiving a complaint from this man. We had a grand talk. He was very apologetic for disturbing my family, and I was very polite. We laughed at the episode. However, my son and his friends did go back and fill in the gully and level off the banking. This was a small penalty to pay for all the many bottles he brought home.

Several times over the years, my son got in minor trouble with the state police. Seems he had the tendency to park his car beside the road and be gone for hours. In the meantime, the state police patrolling the area would wonder what that car was doing being parked for such a long time. My daughter-in-law has received several phone calls from the state police. She has always assured them that it was her husband and commented on what he was doing. Seems my son, when he finds an old dump, will stay, often well after dark, especially if he is having luck.

Once, I remember being at a dump. It was down at the end of an old dirt road that passed directly by a house. When we were done digging and on our way out, the owner of the house was blocking our way out to the main road. Obviously, we stopped. He was very polite and just wanted to know what we were doing. After we explained, he gave us permission to return anytime. In Maine, most of the time, if the property is not posted then people are allowed to hunt, fish, snowmobile, or use the property for other recreational use. A word to the wise, however, is to ask the owner for permission. Most of the time they don't mind as long as you leave the property in as good or better shape than when you found it. In my case, this meant I would fill in any holes that were dug, put fences back up, and thank the owner for the use of his land.

In my hometown there is an old farming section called the Oxbow. It's located in the northwest part of town, and it was and still is great farming country. Years ago, corn was planted on this land to be harvested in Norridgewock for a nearby corn factory. On the property is a very old cemetery and one large old barn still in existence. All the other buildings had long before been destroyed by fire.

A lot of activity used to be enjoyed on the Oxbow. It's called an Oxbow because the land is bounded by the Sandy River. It is the same river that dumps into the Kennebec near the old Norridgewock Native American campsite I referred to before that was destroyed by Captain Malton in 1724.

In the early days of Norridgewock, a family by the name of Waugh owned this property. In fact many of their descendants are buried in the old cemetery. One early 19th century gravestone has a small, hollowed-out section behind what used to be a metal inscription. A story is often told, that bootleggers came across the Sandy River at night and left their "white lightning" or home brew in this gravestone. Those persons wanting this illegal whiskey from a homemade still came to the cemetery, left their money, and took their firewater home. Another story has been told, how the owner of the Oxbow, or his hired hands, hid their old cider or whatever they drank in this old tombstone. When they got thirsty, a trip to the old cemetery quenched their thirst.

There used to be a large set of buildings on the premises, and the owner was fairly wealthy compared to most people at that time. With two corn shops in town, yellow corn was a favorite crop to plant in these many acres making up the Oxbow. This land was alluvial soil in nature, being laid down by the Sandy River's constant flooding. In the fall of the year, this corn was picked by hand and dumped in the middle of the old barn floor. The same barn is still standing today.

After the harvest, an old fashioned corn-husking party was held. People for miles around were invited to come to the party, both men and women. The owner would place or hide a number of red ears of corn in the pile. The object was, if you found a red ear, the lucky person could steal a kiss from his/her date or maybe someone else's date. I'm sure many trips were taken to the old cemetery during the party. After the corn was all husked, a good old-fashioned barn dance was held with country music that long preceded Loretta Lynn and her fame for inventing country music.

Over the years, the farm changed hands, and in the 1940's the property and all the equipment became subject to being liquidated for back taxes. The owner couldn't see how to survive without going bankrupt. One day the owner came up missing. He couldn't be found until someone said let's go down to Oxbow and have another look. Well, they found the poor soul. He had parked his truck down in a hollow that couldn't be seen from the main road. He must have been terribly depressed as he had shot himself in the head.

What's so ironic about this awful tragedy is in a couple of days after he was found, the Federal Government notified his widow a mistake was made. The story continues that he still owed the taxes, but the government was not going to take his property and had offered him a way to pay off his debt without going bankrupt.

A road follows the edge of the Oxbow all the way around the perimeter. By the way, the Oxbow land is shaped like the bow in an oxbow. This land was created as the Sandy River meandered over the years toward the Kennebec. On the backside or northeast side of the Oxbow, there is an old dump. If you're patient and dig long enough and deep enough, you can still find old bottles. For yet another reason, I like to visit the area in the spring during the month of May. This is the season for fiddleheads, and they grow all along the banks of the Sandy River. Fiddleheads are a type of fern, very emerald green in color and very tasty to eat.

These days there has been much to-do about locating the "Old Canada Road." Actually, I think a professor from the University of Maine at Orono is still studying sections of the old road as it makes its way to Canada. This old road linked Canada in the north through Somerset County to Lewiston in the south.

This can be a very interesting historical journey. In the early years of the 19th century, the Maine Legislature appropriated funds to finish construction of this road to link interior Maine to Canada. It was completed in order to accommodate buckboards and rough travel for teams of horses and oxen.

In the early colonial days, oxen were used in both backwoods travel and lumbering. Oxen were easier to take care of than horses. Their stomachs could digest the swale grass and therefore were easier and cheaper to own. Swale grass was found growing naturally in swamps, bogs, and around ponds. Horses could not digest this coarse feed. in addition, cattle from Canada were being driven south to Lewiston or markets in Central Maine.

This road preceded railroads in Maine, let alone in Canada. In Maine history, and the history of Norridgewock, there had been harrowing experiences for early settlers. This section of Maine was a true wilderness in those early years. Both the French settlers moving south from Canada to work in Woolen Mills, and Maine settlers moving ever north to open markets in Canada, experienced tremendous hardships. Lewiston, Maine seems to be the starting point for this road that led north through Cushnoc or present day Augusta, and then on to Winslow, Fairfield, Norridgewock, and eventually Solon, where the old crib work to a bridge that crossed the Kennebec can still be seen. All along this road were taverns used by travelers. A tavern is still located just below where I was brought up, on Route 139 on the road leading to Fairfield to Norridgewock. This was approximately 10 miles from the Danforth Tavern in Norridgewock.

From Norridgewock, traveling north another ten miles brought the traveler to the Jones Tavern, and just beyond this point the road crossed the Kennebec River just below the crib work where the old bridge crossed the Kennebec. Traveling on to Solon there were other stopovers before heading into the towns of Embden, Concord, and Lexington. Eventually the road led to the Bingham Land Grant. The traveler then passed through Pleasant Ridge up a steep mountain into Pierce Pond Township. The road crossed the old Native American trail traveled by Benedict Arnold years earlier on his ill-fated trip to Canada. The road passes between the Kennebec River and East Carry Pond and into the wilderness heading north to west Forks. The old road dropped down over Pierce Mountain and crossed the west branch of the Kennebec before heading up over Johnson Mountain due north through Enchanted, Moose River and finally Canada. The west branch of the Kennebec is now called Dead River. The old crib work or remains of the bridge at West Forks can still be seen today.

The point of this thumbnail sketch description is to provide the reader with an idea of the early activity of the Old Canada Road. It was not meant to provide an accurate historical map of the area. Other sources should be studied for complete accuracy of what went on along the old roadbed!

Old cemeteries can be found all along this road that attest to the early settlers moving back and forth over this part of the country. Just north of Embden Lake, in the township of Lexington, is an old silver mine that can still be seen today. There are old foundations in the town that are still holding treasures waiting to be found. I get a thrill over reminiscing about that old stagecoach and buckboard journey, or just thinking about the ride on horseback traveling to or from Canada on the Old Canada Road. Yes, as I walk sections of it today, I'm always on the lookout for treasure, while I enjoy the adventure that can only be found in the Maine woods.

Remember the old hermit I mentioned earlier who enjoyed bobcat hunting and would start his Blue tick hounds tracking on Dodlin Mountain? Well, let's return to Dodlin Mountain again. Dodlin's underlying strata is granite. Years ago, this granite was shipped all over the state and probably outside the state. I'm told the State Capital Building was built from Dodlin Mountain granite.

At any rate, at the base of the mountain there was a community with houses and barracks to house the men who worked at the granite quarry. I'm sure all of their domestic necessities were brought in by buckboard from local communities. These men were strong, rugged individuals. Many stayed there at the mountain. The work was difficult and dangerous.

Remnants of the old quarry are still present. Great holes cut in the granite can still swallow giant machinery. Huge booms with cables were used to remove giant pieces of granite using iron rods struck by great sledge hammers. If the holes were lined up properly and enough holes were made, the piece of granite would split. Depending on the skill of the workers, a piece could split or break perfectly or it could be ruined.

Like coal miners, the dust from these granite mines was unhealthy for the men. Frankly, the job was highly dangerous. Once the granite slabs were cut and brought out of the holes by the booms, they were swung up to where the teams of horses waited with the special wagons built to carry these huge slabs of granite. The wagons usually were drawn by a two or three team hitch. The wagon had a sling attached to the bottom. It was usually built much higher than a normal wagon. The teamster would drive his wagon over the top of these slabs and a leather sling was placed around the stones. With the help of the sling the granite was raised up off the ground. The teamster would then guide his team down over the mountain to the granite's destination.

Many of the buildings in my hometown have foundations built from this granite, including my own. Years ago the town of Norridgewock was the County Seat for Somerset County. The county jail was totally built from this granite, as were other county buildings. One of those original granite wagons with a sling can still be seen at the State of Maine Museum in Augusta.

Later in the 19th century, when the railroads were pushing into the interior of Maine, granite began to be transported by rail. In the south of Norridgewock, the railroad pushed north from Fairfield into an area known as Hoxies Siding, located close to Martin Stream. At this point, a spur was built Westward across Canada Meadows up to the base of Dodlin Mountain. In hunting deer in this area, I have come across this raised railroad bed. As I remember, it was raised by gravel being hauled in and then dumped in long, narrow mounds. The tracks were laid on top of these mounds.

When I last walked the old railroad bed, it had trees with 10" and 12" diameters growing up through the bed. It's still there, but has long since reverted back to nature. The spur ran from Hoxies Siding through the forest for several miles. Teamsters brought granite down the mountain to the waiting railroad cars, where they were loaded for points south.

In this area was also the location of the community where some of the men lived. This is an area long ignored by bottle hounds, supposedly for good reason. I have walked the area several times while hunting, but have never found a thing. I do have one treasure I found there, however; it is an old porcelain-coated tin cup. I ran across an old spring hole with the remains of a bevel sunk in the ground. Hanging on the limb of an old hemlock tree was this cup. It now hangs in my home.

The last time I saw a cup like this was in an old cider mill in Fairfield Center back in the 1940's. It hung on a nail inside the main door of the old mill beside a huge barrel of fresh cider. The cup was used by any and all persons wanting a drink of cider. As a boy, I would stop in both going and coming to school to drink from that old cup; so did everyone else. By today's health standards, I'm surprised I'm still alive. I can just visualize all those brawny old-timers drinking from this cup to quench their thirst.

There are at least three old roads cutting to the quarry from three different directions. They are still visible and can be followed. The entrance leading off the old Martin Stream Road in Norridgewock, west to Dodlin, appears to have been the most traveled entrance. The road is level and must have been easy for horses to travel. This is the road that leads directly to where the community was located, and it terminates by a wall of granite that spills down over the mountain. If I live long enough, this is the spot I intend to return to and start my search for a dump. Every time I walk into the Dodlin Mountain area, I can smell the history of the location. I can imagine that I hear the banging and clanging of the working men, and my nose tells me there is a dump nearby!

Almost every town when I was a boy had an old-timer who came around selling fresh eggs, milk, cheese, and butter. Norridgewock was no exception. He was a gray-haired old gentleman, and he always came to town with his produce driving a wagon pulled by an old, white horse. He had regular customers and was just as reliable as the clock on the wall in making his deliveries. He was well liked and always stopped at the home my son and daughter-in-law currently own. This was back in the early 1900's, and I believe that at that time his uncle lived in the old house across from mine. He would always stop in about once a week when he came to town.

The old fellow lived on a dirt side-road leading to Bigelow Hill. Years later, after he passed away, I visited the old-timer's home. The first time I ventured out to his property was with a friend. We were going deer hunting, and we drove up this old lane with rock walls on either side and lined with hardwood trees. The lane had been somewhat washed out from neglect. It was an uphill grade, passing through an opening in a rock wall that ran diagonally across the road.

Crossing through the opening, we entered a rolling field that was still very well maintained where hay was still cut. We drove around to find where deer were coming out at night to feed. In driving around, we eventually came to the old homestead. It was located at the top of a hill surrounded by huge sugar maple trees. Again, here was the same New England architecture, "big house, little house, back-house, barn." I may have failed to mention this before, but one reason for this design was to allow the farmer the ability to do his chores without having to go outside during foul weather. It was so much easier to walk out to the barn without having to go outside in a blinding winter blizzard. On this old homestead there was another large barn located in such a way as to create a barnyard. Probably this second barn housed his machinery and excess hay. The barnyard was opened on one side, while fences cordoned off the other two.

In reminiscing about this, it reminds me of the barnyard where I grew up long ago as a boy. I recall one day my step-grandfather had just let his prize bull out in the barnyard and had turned his back to do something. Now my grandfather, like most grandfathers, was a very powerful man. He was Scottish, about six feet tall, weighed 220 pounds, smoked a pipe, and had a huge Roman nose and arms like steel. As he turned back toward the bull, he saw the bull making very angry gestures, such as pawing the ground. My grandfather leaned over and grabbed a wooden stake from the old hayrack. Sure enough, the bull charged my grandfather.

Fred, as I called my grandfather, stepped to the side just as the bull reached him and swung the stake as hard as he could. The stake struck the bull between the eyes and knocked the bull down to the ground. It did not kill the bull, but he went back into the barn rather gingerly. Over the years as a boy, I saw this kind of strength exercised many times by Fred.

Looking around the premises at this other barnyard, it became obvious to me that somewhere around here old bottles could be found. Years later I returned several times for walks with my son, as well as on snowmobile trips.

I remember one such trip up in this area, as I have a picture of my son drinking out of a goat-skinned water bag. He was about 6 years old, it was a beautiful late summer day, and the hay had just been cut; we were just enjoying an outing. On another occasion, we were having a snowmobile ride all over the field. My snowmobile broke down in the field out behind the house. Luck was with us as another snowmobile rider came along and gave us a lift to the nearest telephone. We called for help and got out of our predicament.

Many years later, my son and I revisited this pristine place and were rewarded. The old place was still standing and an observer would notice its entrance points south, away from the prevailing winds. In walking around the house, it was easy to locate the back door leading off the kitchen. This was the spot where the lady of the house hung out her clothes to dry. An old well hole is also there. Just beyond the well hole was an old, stone wall that we began to follow. The wall led north of the house through a few old apple trees and seemed to block off a pasture from a field located in the northwest corner of the property.

Sure enough a few yards from the back door, we began to find old glass in the rock wall. As we moved stones, we began to locate old bottles. There were cone inks, Dr. Pierce's Favorite Prescription and Remedy, old whiskies, small drug bottles, and several others.

We worked hard for the rest of the day and came home with several new bottles. "New," in that we did not have any of them in our old bottle collection. My old bottle digging knowledge tells me there are still more bottles in this location. Behind the house there was an old wagon road leading to a back field. It led through some old grapevines over a small, wet hole and crossed between an opening in another rock wall into what we used to call the "back forty." The left side of this field sloped down and dropped off steeply into a hardwood ridge. This would be a perfect spot for the old farmer to drive his white horse and wagon loaded with trash and dump the trash over this bank. One day I will return to this "back forty" because my nose tells me there are other old treasures to be found there.

Let's jump around a little more in Somerset County. We'll start west of the Kennebec River in two old lumbering towns called Skinner and Loweltown, move down to Rangeley in the Western Mountains, and then travel southeast to Martin Stream in Norridgewock. Skinner and Loweltown are located deep in the wilderness of northwestern Maine. I mention their names as I'm sure it would still be an adventure to visit these places. Also, I'm sure a four wheel drive would have to be used to travel the old roads. At the turn of the century, there was a railroad station with several houses and camps where the lumber men lived.

Most of the area in this section of Maine is still uninhabited and is unorganized territory. Such names as

Dead River, Enchanted, Ten Thousand Acres, Spencer Lake, Holeb Falls and the Bow trip by canoe are just a few of the name places in this region. For a terrific history of the region, I refer the reader to *The Kennebec Wilderness Awakens*, by Mary Calvert. Someday I'm going to visit these ghost towns, as sure enough there must be treasures to find. As a point of interest, during World War II, this general area was home to a prisoner of war camp that was located in the Moose River region.

Moving south to the town of Rangley, my family and I spent two years living among the residents there. I was the town's Superintendent of Schools during the construction of the new Rangley Lakes Regional School. During my stay, I located several old dumps. A couple of old bottles are still in my collection that came from Rangley. One was a very old hand painted "Old Spice" bottle, the other is a druggist bottle with the name Rangley, Maine, embossed in the glass. As a point of interest, my collection reflects about seventy druggist bottles from different towns in Maine.

Now we will move south to Martin Stream. I once came across an octagonally-shaped log cabin way back in the forest. It must have been used by an old trapper. The cabin is in ruins today. I found no bottles at this site, but I mention it because of its beauty and location. It's the sort of spot I can't stay away from, so I visit it often. It is located on a rise overlooking Martin Stream, and it is surrounded by tall, straight white pine trees. There is no underbrush in the area, and the forest floor is covered with thick, moist, green moss. You actually sink over your ankles in this cool setting. A spring hole is located not far from the cabin for drinking water. I often visit this magical wonderland to regenerate my love of nature.

The town that used to be the location of an old fort sits at the confluence of the Sabasticook and Kennebec River is our next trip. The town that is located there now is Winslow, Maine. Old Fort Halifax was located at the angle where these two rivers merge, and an old blockhouse still stands on the site. A friend of the family accompanied my son and me to his Aunt Mary's home, an old Victorian era house located in Winslow. Just behind the house were several large rocks that were in the middle of a field. This is where the lady walked out behind the house and dumped her rubbish.

The field was grown over with years of natural cover. Digging was easy, and many treasures were found in this dump. I'm simply going to name a few of the wonderful old bottles we found there: Buffalo Lithia Water, Bunker Hill Pickles, Atwood's' Bitters, cone inks, including two blue inks, two horseshoe flasks, a quart size whiskey flask, Dr. Kennedy's Favorite Prescription, Dana's Sarsaparilla, several Dr. Kilmer's Swamp Root, Saratoga Mineral Springs Congress Water, Moxie Nerve Food, and canning jars of different sizes including some with bail lids, several Mason's Patent Nov. 30th 1858 with zinc lids, many American Anodyne Lineament bottles, Dr. Hostetter's Stomach Bitters, Pure Olive Oil, many unembossed medicine bottles in various colors and Mrs. S.A. Allen's Worlds Hair Restorer. These bottles are just a few uncovered on this terrific adventure. As I recall, we came home after several visits with many, many treasures. What a memory!

While down this way, lets travel to the town of Sidney's Boat Landing. One day my son and I put the boat in the Kennebec River at Sidney. We were going to check out the banks of the river for old dumps. It was a gorgeous day, the river was calm, and everything was just fine. We were going down river toward Augusta, the state capital, a trip of about five miles. Puttering along, we enjoyed watching several ducks with their families swimming along the shore. Periodically, a fish would surface. In this area of the river, several bald eagles could be seen soaring and looking very majestic with their white head and tail feathers.

This is also a beautiful section of the river with high, steep banks on either side. The river is wider below Sidney than it is up by Norridgewock, or at least it used to be when the Edwards Dam was still in place in Augusta. Since the dam has been removed, the water level has dropped considerably thus narrowing the river bed.

After an hour or so we looked on the west shore and there was a dog lying on the bank. We didn't think much of it and continued on our trip. Finally, we spotted what appeared to be an old dump on the west side of the river. It was high up on a very steep bank that fell to the water. The bank was covered with hardwood trees and evergreen trees at the very top of the bank.

We pulled the boat to shore, wrapped the anchor rope around some alders, got out of the boat, and looked almost straight up the bank. The dump was close to the top of this steep climb. We started out clawing our way up through the trees. In places, it was almost vertical, and this made for very slow going.

Once we arrived at the site, my son went up first and then I brought up the rear: We found that we struggled to dig as the site was at such a slant. I could hardly stand up. We slipped and slid, and if we were not extremely careful, we could have tumbled down the bank right into the river. We found several bottles. My favorite was a bottle embossed with the words, "Bowditch Webster and Company, City Drugstore under Cony House, Augusta, Maine." What's interesting is the old Cony House was raised at least 150 years ago. It was a landmark in Augusta before the turn of the 20th century and tourists visited this old structure for well over one hundred years.

Another bottle was embossed with the words, "Fuller Drugstore, Established 1819, Augusta, Maine." There were other finds as well, one of which was a 4" tall, amber pill bottle.

We left the site late in the day and headed back to the Sidney Boat Landing. On our way back up the river, we spotted the same dog still on the edge of the bank, and again we still didn't think much about it. A week or so later we decided to revisit this same dump. As we came down the river for the second time, that dog was still in the same location. We dug in the same dump and would you believe it, I found an amber glass stopper. My son said, "Dad, I think that stopper will fit that amber pill bottle you found last week."

When we left the dump this time we had that dog on our mind. We sensed something was wrong. As we neared the dog's location, we moved the boat very close to the dog. It now became obvious something was wrong. The dog was thin and appeared to be blind. From the look of the immediate surroundings we could see the dog had been there for some time. All we had for food was an apple, and I tossed it over by the dog. He sniffed around, found the apple and gulped it down.

Since a dog in this predicament could possibly be rabid, we decided not to touch him, but instead called the Animal Control Officer when we arrived home. We were assured the Augusta Animal Control Officer would return our call after checking out our directions. A day later, he phoned us back. They had found the dog. It was a Bullmastiff, and it was both blind and deaf. It had fallen down over some ledges and had been missing for several weeks. The control officer was persistent, and he finally located the owner. The dog's name was Vinnie, and he was reunited with his owner. By the way, the amber glass stopper did fit the bottle, and the bottle with its stopper now sits on my kitchen windowsill.

There are times when I wonder why there are so many old country roads, especially when many of them are now discontinued. In their time, these old roads were in settled areas that were later abandoned. Maybe these early settlers were burned out, or maybe the last generation simply died out. Whatever the reason, whole neighborhoods simply disappeared.

I recall visiting one night a neighborhood off the East Ridge Road in Cornville. While exploring the long ridge many years ago, I walked down an old tote road, crossed a long section of corduroy road, and entered an opening. This opening apparently had been a neighborhood, as there were several old, fallen down buildings visible, including two homesites with only foundations left.

Following the washed-out road, I came to the edge of the Weserunsett Stream. Evidently the road had once crossed the stream as there were the remains of an old bridge. Granite abutments were on either side, with two long stringers spanning the stream. A few old boards still held the stringers together. It appeared to me, these remnants were the remains of an old covered bridge.

I did not cross the stream, but instead turned my attention back toward the old houses and the fields. Everything had pretty much reverted back to nature. The fields were covered with golden rod and alders. One field had been plowed in the past as the furrows were still visible. A couple of old buildings were still being used by hunters as they waited undercover for deer to approach several old apple trees in the area.

These same buildings were home to a family of porcupine as their droppings and signs of ever present gnawing were apparent.

Several old bottles were found on the bank of the stream; however, this trip I brought my fishing rod and managed to catch a few nice brook trout. Before leaving this secluded spot, I remember sitting down and trying to determine who these people were, and where they went. The answer could probably be found in the history of Cornville. As I contemplated this peaceful setting, it came to me that these people probably were born, lived here, and eventually died, thus leaving their property to revert back to nature. This is as it should be, as when these people settled here, they carved their livelihood from nature, and therefore it's now going back to nature.

I left this neighborhood with pleasant thoughts of visiting a sort of memorial to those who had lived there many years ago. In thinking of this trip and the old, dilapidated bridge, I'm reminded that I did not cross the stream and follow the old road to the west. I must return to satisfy my curiosity! Are there other buildings across the stream? Is there an old dump hidden in the forest? Where does the old road lead? Why was there a bridge crossing to the west? You can have so much fun hypothesizing about the past generations.

The old Ferry Road is another country road that supported a long lost neighborhood. It's located just off the Middle Road that leads to Skowhegan from

Fairfield. It is in Fairfield and runs east to Hinkley, just south of the Somerset/Kennebec County line.

I have parked my truck on the Middle Road and walked the length of this country road. As you enter the road, it leads down a long, sloping hill. On either side are stone walls with split-rails built onto the walls. Years ago, holes were drilled into the rocks and iron rods were inserted into these holes. Next, the builder drilled holes into split–rails, and these were placed over the iron rods. This procedure left a rather elaborate fence, one that remained for well over one hundred and fifty years.

As you near the end of the slope, on the right hand side of the road is a rather large bog. On several occasions, I have walked up onto moose wading in the murky water eating lily pads. it is such a joy to observe these creatures in the wild doing what comes naturally. People in general are missing a wondrous sight, if they have never seen a moose feeding with its head submerged underwater. Upon raising its majestic head, water is flowing off and weeds and grass are dangling from its mouth. If you're lucky, it will be a bull with great horns. As the animal looks around, its huge ears flap and it shakes its head to help dissipate the water as the huge nostrils flare and the "bell" on its neck under the chin flaps with the movement.

Moving on, the road starts up a steep hill lined with hemlock. On the left is a ditch that is washed out from years of draining the hill. Also, the road has washed out in sections making it hard to maneuver.

Probably it's a mile or more to the top of the hill that leads to several foundations.

On the way up the road, I began to see old glass in the ditch. This was encouraging because this glass probably was washed out from an old dump. Sure enough, on topping the hill the first foundation came into view, with the ever-present remains of old lilac bushes. To the left of the foundation, where the ground pitches off to the west, was a small dump. The dump produced three or four old whiskies and a lot of old broken glass.

As the distance from the truck was a couple of miles and it was getting late, I decided to just walk the length of the road instead of spending all my time digging. I felt to explore this whole area was more important than spending my time in one place. Walking along, I came to three more foundations that I noted in my memory. Someday I would return to this phantom neighborhood and spend time digging, instead of walking.

From all indications, this area was a farming neighborhood, and it had once been rather prosperous. The homes were large, and the barns were twice as large as the homes. Old farming equipment could be seen on the edge of the grown-up fields. It was as though the people just simply walked off one day, never to return. One day I shall return and try to uncover more of this mystery.

It's interesting to note that the remnants of an old dump can actually speak to you after all of its years of silence. For example, if you find many medicine bottles, its possible one of the owners was sickly. Couple this with several whiskies and maybe another resident had a drinking problem. Once, I found a dump with many, many American Anodyne Liniment bottles. This family had a lot of aches and pains, and physically probably worked extremely hard. Old clay pipes tell you they enjoyed tobacco, and many old Bromo Seltzer bottles indicate someone had a very poor stomach. Ink bottles reflect that the family, at least a member of the family, was literate. Some old dumps had many old inks of various sizes and shapes, indicating much writing was enjoyed. Anyway, I left this old country neighborhood with every intention of returning. One day, I will!

Today it's common to observe young people as well as older people walking the highways and byways looking for cans and bottles. This trash may be returned to a recycling center for money. A bottle hound does the same thing, only not on the road. Instead, the bottle hound will move back ten yards or so and look closely for old metal protruding out of the ground.

This can be rewarding. In my area of Somerset County, I try to locate the oldest roads, roads that were once traveled by stagecoaches, buckboards or once were paths following rivers. Many times I have parked my truck on one end and walked back to the other side. Bigelow Hill Road was one such area I walked. I located several good areas along this road that were productive. It appears to me that a wagon had passed by and a pail was tossed out filled with old cultch. Usually these are not dumps, but just small deposits. This procedure of walking the roadways is excellent physical activity and can be well worthwhile.

A helpful hint for someone starting out to become a bottle hound is to start looking for dumps in early spring or late fall. In early spring the trees are bare and the earth is soft. Also, you can see long distances in the forest. It may be a little wet, so boots are a necessity, but generally the spring of the year is the best time to go for long adventuresome walks. At this time of year, just locate a site and return to it at a later time.

The fall of the year is another good time to scout around. Trees have shed their leaves and vegetation has stopped growing. Again, you can see long distances. There are drawbacks in the fall, however, as the ground is considerably harder than in the spring. Another problem in the fall is it is hunting season. Make sure you wear your florescent orange clothing. Safety is always in style when wandering around in the Maine woods.

My son has always maintained he could find a bottle in a dump that has previously been dug. The Skowhegan dump was no exception. This dump had been dug and redug over the years. Many bottle diggers had been successful. Stories have been told of finding historical flasks and other very expensive bottles. For many years, we ignored this dump because of its availability to others, and because we knew it had been visited many times by other bottle hounds.

MESSAGE IN A BOTTLE

One day, out of curiosity, my son decided to visit this dump and see first-hand where all these treasures came from. Boy, are we glad he did!

First, I'll describe this huge dump. As you walk onto the site, small alders block your way. You have to thread your way through these closely grown bushes that are about 10 feet tall. The land slopes down to a wet hole that at one time was a small brook. Even now, if it rains for an extended period of time, the brook will fill up and run downhill toward an old cemetery.

Between the brook and the alders is a very old, huge, dead, willow tree. From observation, I would say the willow grew right in the middle of the dump. New sprouts always appear in the spring. Having grown in a wet hole, the old tree was almost impossible to destroy. Years ago someone had cut it down; the diameter of the stump is probably eight feet, with a root system that spreads out thirty feet or more.

From the old trash surrounding the stump and its roots, the dump could be dated from the middle of the 19th century to the turn of the 20th. It had been dug many times as hummocks of unearthed trash extended out for approximately forty feet in all directions.

The first time my son dug here, he was rewarded many times over. It's important to make the reader aware of his state of mind when digging. Most bottle diggers scratch the surface or maybe dig down a foot or so. My son finds a likely spot and totally destroys it. If he thinks a bottle is under his feet, he will dig down until the bottom of the dump has been reached. Sometimes this could be as deep as five or six feet. I have seen him dig holes that were similar to caves. He actually has slid into these caves on his back and dug over his head. You would think he was excavating a trench to lay a foundation. Dirt flies through the air as he digs, every piece of glass broken or not is studied, and if you're in his way you will be buried.

Most bottle hounds do not work at their hobby. He not only works at it, he enjoys it. He has the strength, perseverance, determination and knowledge of where he is digging that allows him to locate treasures never before detected by others. At one time we made a good team, but my years have slowed me down. Now I dig, but I laugh at my meager efforts compared to his. If he can't move something that is in his way, he'll dig around it, break it, cut it, bend it, saw it, or find some way to move it out of his way. For these efforts, he has been rewarded many times by locating valuable treasures.

On this first trip to the Skowhegan dump, he came home with beautiful old inks, including blue inks, a couple of historical flasks, numerous household bottles, whiskies, soda, and miscellaneous bottles. Obviously, many more trips were taken to this site. Once, I remember digging under a huge root and pulling out bottle after bottle. All our tools were used in this dump; however, a bow saw was the most useful in cutting through the roots. On another occasion, my son was digging in sloppy, gooey mud as it had rained considerably a day or so earlier. Again, he was rewarded!

It must be pointed out to the reader, my son's clothing always showed his desire to locate bottles. Nothing would stop him. He would be filthy, caked with dirt, and dripping with water, sweat, and sometimes blood. His face was usually coated with dirt and streaked with sweat as it cascaded off his chin. I hated to see him head for my truck and learned to always take an old drop cloth or something for him to sit on beside my seat.

To this day, we still visit this dump and have never been disappointed. This site is an excellent example of my son's belief that he could find a bottle in a previously dug dump. So often over the years this belief has proved to be true.

The next adventure takes place in the town of Sidney, Maine. It began like any other family outing with my son, his wife, and their two children. They had taken a picnic lunch and planned to spend the day simply enjoying a beautiful fall day in the Maine woods. The family had not planned where they were going. An old cemetery far down in a field caught their eye. This appeared to be a nice, quiet place to enjoy an afternoon.

A long dirt road gracefully divided well kept fields on either side, as it terminated at the entrance to the old cemetery. Driving down the road, the family took note of the gravestones. Once they stopped, they became aware of an old road that led down a hill, apparently leading the traveler toward the banks of the Kennebec River.

After visiting the well kept cemetery and enjoying their picnic, they decided to explore the other road. It was a clear, crisp fall day, and the leaves were falling off the hardwood trees in the forest. Climbing over an old, wooden gate, the family began to slowly walk through the leaves and follow the road that curved to the right ever closer to the river. They had to climb over some old blow-downs, and they moved through the woods over a hardwood ridge. It apparently was easier walking.

Moving along they eventually came to the brim of a steep ravine that cut across their path. Looking down the slope and through the trees, a small brook could be seen with water tumbling over rocks, creating small, dammed-up pools as it moved toward the river. Slowly and methodically each member of the family started down over the ravine. They reached the bottom and carefully began to move up the brook.

As they moved, all the creatures of the woods were well aware of the human presence. They heard the chattering of red squirrels as they seemed to scold the intruders and the piercing cry of a crow warning all woodland creatures of danger. Here and there a bird would dart in and grab an insect before swiftly flying back up into the tree top. Couple all of these natural noises with the sound of running water flowing over rocks and the sound of falling leaves; it must have been a glorious day. The smell of the forest and all the mysterious odors associated with it added another dimension of peacefulness. I'm sure my family was enjoying every minute of their developing adventure.

Moving to what appeared to be a cow pasture they began to see remnants of old farm machinery: wooden wheels, parts of old iron wagons, and old buckets sticking out of the ground. The ravine began to rise up into a field, and the sides terminated at the base of a huge pine tree. It was my daughter-in-law who first recognized they were in the midst of an old dump. My son began to dig and unearthed several treasures. From this point on, I will refer to this location as "the dump." This dump became a bottle digger's paradise and coughed up treasures of such magnitude as to stagger anyone's mind.

My son and his family brought home pails full of bottles. They couldn't wait to share their experience with me. I took one look at their treasures and my jaw dropped to the ground. "Where did you find these?" I stuttered as I held a black glass whiskey with a pontil in my hand. Their experience was related to me, and I listened with wide eyes and an excitement that was bubbling over with enthusiasm. "When can we go back to your dump?"

It was a couple of weeks before I had time to go. In the meantime, my son returned several times and always came home with many, many bottles. I was afraid the dump would be cleaned out before I would have a chance to find just one bottle.

One day he was gone so long his wife and everybody else began to worry. It was way after dark, and he should have been home long ago. My daughter-in-law's telephone rang; it was the state police calling to see if she owned a car that had been parked beside the road in Sidney most of the day. She assured them it was her husband and indicated what he was doing. The state police were concerned primarily because he had parked on the side of the road in a dip. Drivers coming or going couldn't see his car until they were right on top of it. It all worked out and he returned home later on in the evening with his usual cache.

One Saturday, he and I were off to Sidney. On the way I was told of the dump and how difficult it was to dig. We traveled the same path as my son's family had weeks before when I observed the dump for the first of many times. I was stunned. My son had destroyed the end of the dump closest to the pine tree. The only thing stopping progress was a huge pine root. My son had burrowed beneath the root as far as he could, but it was obvious the root had to come out.

On this day, however, we did not have a saw. So we began to dig on the backside of the root. This earth we were digging in was extremely hard. I'm sure it was clay that had been bulldozed over the dump. Progress was extremely slow. The iron and the old farm machinery buried over the old dump didn't help. We were doing more pulling and bending then digging. Slowly we were able to scratch away a few inches of clay.

The next procedure was to begin making a trench across the width of the dump. Finally, we were able to start a trench, and both of us climbed into it and began methodically to widen the area. Every now and then one of our diggers would clink onto glass and out would come a bottle. The trench got deeper and deeper and finally my son began to dig a hole straight down and eventually laid down on his back and started digging over his head. We would switch off in relief to rest.

It is difficult to dig below your head in a partially upside down position. Blood moves to your head and the result is light-headedness. After a period of time, we were resting, and my son was scratching around under the lip of the hole. He couldn't see it, but he heard metal against glass. He was very careful; he stopped scratching and reached down under the lip and felt the bottle.

He began to dig with his fingers. I was sitting in the dirt watching him maneuver his arm and hand in the hole. He looked at me and said, "This bottle is stuck solid in the clay. I can feel the side of the bottle and some embossing." He continued to dig and finally said, "I think I know what it is."

Like an expectant father, I retorted, "Well, what is it?"

He withdrew his arm and said, "Feel and tell me what you think?" I reached down and could touch the bottle. I had no idea what it was but knew from his face the bottle was a great treasure. He finally said, "Dad, I think that bottle is an historical flask!"

We both held our breath as he continued to dig with his fingers. We were hoping the bottle was whole and not broken. He asked me for my pocket knife and began to whittle the clay surrounding the bottle. It moved! Reaching in, he removed the bottle and kept it out of my sight as he studied his prize. Looking at me he said, "It's a Masonic historical flask!"

With that, he handed the flask to me. It was a beautiful dark green with Masonic designs embossed in the glass, with an open pontil on the base. We laughed and I hollered, and I congratulated him on his treasure. We shook hands and acted like a couple of teenagers. For the rest of the afternoon, we could barely manage to keep our eyes off this beautiful flask. Obviously, we did manage somehow, as when it came time to go home we had filled several old pails with antique bottles. The flask was placed inside my son's shirt for total protection.

This was a wonderful adventure. We experienced everything necessary for a perfect day. A few days later, we returned with all the necessary tools, including a saw to remove that pesky pine root.

On this second trip we hit a gold mine of bottles. I'm hesitant to say, "You name it, we found it," but we started early in the morning and stayed all day. We had approximately one hundred bottles, and we decided to walk out through a pasture instead of the ravine. Each of us was loaded down as we headed toward the truck. My left leg was aching and causing me discomfort.

Shortly, over a rise in the pasture, we faced another steep ravine. My son went down over the side with his load of bottles. I just couldn't make it loaded down, so he came back, took my load, and I slid down on my rump. Once we climbed the other side, I decided to leave the bottles I had, walk up through this next field to the truck, and drive back to where we came out of the ravine.

As I recall, the hay was a second growth, as it was about a foot tall and very green. I reached the truck just as it was getting dark. In driving down across the field, I put my headlights on to pick the best path to follow. We loaded the bottles in the truck, climbed in, and found ourselves in a stuck truck. The grass was so green and therefore wet, that my tires just spun. We both got out, I put the truck in low gear, and we both began to push.

By this time, the farmer at the end of the road had come out, and he began to walk toward us. Before he got very far, however, with one mighty heave, my son got the truck started, and I managed to keep it going until reaching the gravel road that led to the cemetery. As we approached the main road, the farmer stepped out to stop us.

He was cordial; he only wanted to know what we were doing. My son told him we were bird hunting down by the river. This was logical, as I had my shotgun in the front seat. That seemed to satisfy him and we were on our way home.

Driving home we decided that, next time when we returned to the dump, we would use our boat. It could be put in the river at the Sidney Boat Landing. We could use our "Golden Oldie", ten horsepower, 1956 Johnson motor to take us up the river. Arriving at the spot, we would simply pull the boat up on shore and walk up the draw to the dump. One must remember that my son continued to visit this treasured spot between my visits. He always came home with more bottles. This went on for several years.

Once, probably on a weekend, we hooked up the old 12' aluminum boat with my Golden Oldie and headed for Sidney. We arrived at the boat landing and put the boat into the water. It was a gorgeous day, and I remember a man and his dog were playing in a ballpark adjacent to the landing. We watched for awhile as the man threw a frisbee and the dog ran after it, snagged it in the air, and returned it to his master.

This man and his dog could very well have been on a television show I saw several years ago. I guess the point of the show was for the owner of the dog to contort himself into as many shapes as possible and fire the frisbee as fast and as far as he could. The dog's part was to jump as high as he could, catch the frisbee, and return it to the owner as many times as possible without failure, in a given amount of time.

Anyway, we enjoyed the show and finally climbed in the boat, started the motor, and headed up the river. We had to watch the left shoreline closely for the right ravine, where it directed the brook into the river. About four miles up river, we spotted a sandbar where the deposits of silt had been laid down by a brook. We pulled in to the sandbar and docked the boat by wrapping the anchor chain around some alders.

MESSAGE IN A BOTTLE

Taking our tools, including a pick ax, we headed up the draw. It was rocky and meandered up through the forest. The sides were steep, covered with hemlock trees, and difficult to climb. Primarily, we stuck to the bottom of the draw, jumping from rock to rock. Slowly we made our way up through the cool, shadowy, wet ravine for about half a mile. As we rounded a corner, there was the location where we had come down over the banking several weeks before. Just ahead was "The Dump."

Arriving at the site, I could see more of the dump had been destroyed. Climbing under a barbed wire fence, I once again stood at the edge of "The Dump." We studied the area, put our tools down, and began to scratch, dig, pull, push, and in general claw our way deeper into the earth. As we moved even deeper, bottles began to show up in the clay. Sometimes, we would have to whittle the dirt around the bottle to dislodge it. I brought a camera on this trip and some wonderful shots were taken of this procedure. One photograph shows the bottom of the hole with a bottle embedded in the dirt. The picture shows my son whittling the dirt.

Again, we switched off in the hole, as it wasn't big enough for both of us to dig. On one of my turns I hit glass and uncovered a Golden Bitters bottle. Alas, as I whittled the dirt away from the sides, the bottle came loose and the back was broken off. Looking at the bottle before it came loose, I had thought it was whole.

Yes, we experienced disappointment on many of our journeys. This reminded me of a Suffolk Pig Bitters bottle I once found in a Norridgewock dump. It was laying about eye level in an area I was digging. Everyone on this trip came over to watch me pluck "the pig" out of the stratified earth. Using my fingernails, I pried the ends and out popped a broken Pig Bitters. It had looked whole laying in the bank where I was digging. This was the second time a very valuable bottle had eluded me. Oh well, maybe next time the bottle will be intact.

We spent the day finding old bottles and laying them around the base of the old pine. The old pine was now about ten feet behind us as we dug up the end of the draw. Walking out to the boat that evening, we were loaded down with bottles and tools.

By the way, this was the trip I took a pick ax to help break through the clay. As I mentioned earlier, my son told me not to use it for fear of breaking a bottle. I didn't listen, and I swung the pick ax down through an old pail and right through an historical flask. The flask was in the pail. As I took the pick ax home that evening, I wanted to throw it overboard. Never again have I suggested using a pick!

Many times we have returned to "The Dump" and always came home with a treasure. "The Dump" is still in Sidney and still produces bottles. Now and then we return to dig and renew old memories.

What is it that makes old bottles so interesting to people and to me specifically? For one thing, each bottle is unique. Before the invention of the automatic bottle machine in 1903, each bottle had a neck that was more or less handmade. The rule of thumb in dating a bottle is that the lower the seam, the older the bottle. For example, if the seam from the mold goes through the lip of a bottle, it was made after 1903. If the seam is half way up the neck, the bottle can be dated to about 1880-1900. If the seam is located on the shoulder, it can be dated from 1850-1880. Some bottles have no seam. These are called "turn in the mold bottles." The glassblower simply turned the bottle in the mold to eliminate any sign of the mold seam.

Most old bottles were blown by a glassblower into a mold. The glassblower simply took his blowpipe, dipped it into molten blobs, then "blew" it into the shape of the mold. A careful glassblower could shape a section of the neck almost up to the lip. Once the neck was formed and the glass had cooled, the mold was then opened, the bottle taken out, and the lip made onto the neck.

The glassblower then used other tools to form the lip. It could be what was called a "blob top," which was simply a blob of molten glass wrapped around the neck and then smoothed. Or, it could be a flared lip, where the glassblower simply pulled the lip and neck into shape. Another method was to place some molten glass on a rod and simply bead it onto the neck. Sometimes a bottle has a sheared lip. This kind of lip gives the appearance the neck was never completed, and it sometimes has rough shaped edges. Most all of these necks accepted a cork stopper. The A.B.M. (automatic bottle machine) created a lip that looked like a crown and accepted a metal cap. This type of metal cap is still used today. Other methods were used to make applied lips, but generally these were the standard procedures.

On the bottom of pre-civil war blown bottles there were fractures called pontils. The pontil mark was made when the glassblower broke the iron rod off the base of the bottle just before it had completely cooled. The earliest pontils were jagged and sharp glass. As the procedure developed, the blower learned to polish the rough edges and smooth the end of the bottle. Eventually, a snap case was invented and the need for an iron rod was eliminated.

Inside the mold, a customer could request any lettering or picture he/she would want pressed right into the bottle. It was called embossing. The mold was sometimes especially made for the customer. It could be raised in relief or sunken into the glass. These bottles are prized. A bottle digger can tell what the bottle was used for as well as what the contents were. Many bottles had no embossing, but originally had a gummed, paper label. Over time these labels were simply worn off or destroyed.

Some of the most prized bottles were made in a mold shaped like an object. For example, the mold for the Suffolk Pig Bitters was shaped like a pig. The National Ear of Corn Bitters was shaped like an ear of corn, and the Brown's Celebrated Indian Bitters was shaped like a Native American.

A Bitters bottle is a classification. Bitters was the name of a medicine. It seems in the 18th century gin was being taxed. To get around the tax, the salesman added some herbs and called it medicine. Later in the 19th century this mixture became known as Bitters. It was a strong alcoholic beverage that became very popular in America. The ladies of the house, including grandmothers, seemed to enjoy the Bitters remedy.

There are many classifications of bottles. Some are: Avon, Bakers, Beam, Beer, Candy Containers, Coca-Cola, flasks, decanters, fruit jars, inks, pickle, sarsaparilla and kinds of soda, to name a few. There are others, including milk and poisons.

There are scholarly books that list and define these classifications. A visit to your public library will enlighten the inquiring mind. Also, there are publications such as newspapers, newsletters, magazines, and bottle clubs both national and state, as well as auctions available to the reader.

It apparently was easier to ask for a specific Bitters recipe than to request a bottle of gin. I'm sure most of the health problems suffered by the ladies were either cured or dulled. After a few drinks of Bitters, they probably forgot they were ever sick or ill.

Another famous and very valuable bottle is the historical flask. These flasks were embossed with famous figures such as a silhouette of President George Washington, Thomas Jefferson, or Lafayette and Liberty. Hundreds of styles were made, and they can be extremely rare. Most flasks were decorated. Some collectors concern themselves with only flasks. For greater knowledge on historical flasks I refer the reader to the book, *American Bottles and Flasks*, by

Helen McKearin and Kenneth McWilson. Again, flasks, like bottles, contained an alcoholic beverage, usually whiskey.

Wandering through the forests of Maine, there have been two environmental issues that have bothered me greatly. The first is the destruction of the wilderness through clear-cutting. Over the years, I have traveled north on several occasions to the Canadian Province of Quebec. On a fishing trip to northern Quebec, I observed clear-cutting at its worst. Whole mountains were bald with brush bulldozed into ravines. I drove for miles on dirt roads owned by the Park Service of Quebec and saw forests completely destroyed.

It appears the further north one drives from Central Maine, the more clear-cutting becomes evident. The Maine wilderness has always meant a great deal to me, but clear-cutting is slowly destroying this Maine treasure. There are organizations fighting to help preserve our forests for future generations. My fondest hope and prayer is that the Maine wilderness will not become devastated like sections of northern Quebec.

The second environmental issue I'm very concerned with is the apparent neglect of blow-downs. Specifically, poplar trees appear to be easily blown over or uprooted in many sections of Maine. Just a few days ago, I was in an area of the forest with a huge cover of poplar. Hundreds of cords of poplar were lying uprooted on the forest floor. This was over an extended area and the trees crisscrossed each other. It's my understanding, poplar logs are now being used by the paper companies to make quality paper. If this is a fact, why do private forest owners ignore their forests by letting these blow-downs rot where they lay?

Back in the 1970's, someone who had been a bottle digger said to me, "Most dumps have already been dug," the indication being that no more old bottles could be found. This is a false assumption. My son, friends, and family have proven this to be false. This book is a testament to what is still out there for bottle treasure hunters. In thirty years of enjoying my hobby, I have covered a very small area of Maine in hunting for old, forgotten foundations and old dumps. Simply put, the surface has just barely been scratched. Often I think of the thousands of bottles still hidden in Maine, let alone all of New England.

I'm saddened to think my adventures in the wilderness are growing shorter. My only real pleasure is knowing my son will continue the hobby. He is smitten with the spirit of being a bottle hound. Not too long ago, he touched me deeply when he gave me a special bottle as a present and thanked me for introducing him to the hobby of collecting old bottles for enjoyment.

Speaking of my son reminds me of his backyard. The reader may recall he lives in an old, New England Cape, circa 1786. One day he was out behind the back-house next to the building. He had seen old glass and broken bottles; he decided to explore further. He went into the barn, got a spade, and returned to the area of the lawn to be dug. I'm sure his wife didn't know what he was about to do. At any rate, he began to dig and bottles began to appear.

Like I did in my own lawn out behind the barn, he found bottle after bottle. I remember one was a beautiful, emerald green Congress Mineral Spring Water bottle. My granddaughter and he came rushing over to my place to let me know of their treasure. I was surprised and elated. When they went home, I was with them and enjoyed their enthusiasm and excitement. He has a curio cabinet with only his most valuable bottles on display. Many of those found behind his back-house are in this cabinet.

My leg began to bother me on one particular trip to "The Dump." It became a serious problem. Eventually, I had bypass surgery to an artery, and a plastic artery was implanted in my leg. In the recovery process, I had to walk miles to strengthen the muscles. This walking generated this next adventure.

Most people walk along the highway swinging their arms for exercise, or they have an exercise treadmill. I guess I march to a different drummer. Down the road where I live is an old tote road that meanders through the forest. My truck can negotiate this road. When I want to go for a walk, I drive back into the woods and walk out to an old country road between the town of Fairfield and Norridgewock. The road runs east and west, and is approximately three miles long. From where I park the truck to the end of the road and back is about four miles. This is an excellent walk to strengthen your legs and give your cardiovascular system a good work out.

I walk this area because of the enjoyment and (you probably guessed it) because there are several old foundations along the way. Also, this is an area where I hunt during deer season. There are several deer stands, and the area is absolutely beautiful. Walking along the old dirt road, the animals become evident through observing their tracks.

One day while walking, I saw some brush move, and it looked like the whole forest was moving. Stopping, I saw a large, cow moose with twins who stepped out into the road. They had been lying down when I disturbed their nap. If the reader has never seen a moose, I'll describe one as follows: they are so homely they are beautiful. The calves will stay with their mother for two years before moving off on their own. From the size of these twins, I would say they were about ready to leave.

There have been days when I would simply climb up into a deer stand and just watch for wildlife. It's a terrific way to enjoy one's surroundings. One stand in particular is about ten feet from the ground and overlooks a swale hole or meadow. The stand is in a pine tree, and I can see for several hundred yards in both directions of a stream that runs through the meadow. At one end of the stream, it's dammed up by a family of beavers. Their actions are a joy to observe.

Sitting there listening to the wind move through the pine branches is refreshing. It reminds me of when I was a boy so many years ago. I had a friend who played the harmonica. We used to climb to the top of pine trees and sway in the wind while he played his tunes.

Usually, I do walk the four miles. I'm always checking the old foundations for treasures. At the end of the walk to the west, the road terminates at a washed-out bridge that used to cross Martin Stream. On either side of the road are sand dunes. Close to the washed-out bridge is a foundation. Long ago, the building was destroyed by fire. An old road can still be seen leading up a small hill and entering into a large dune. On both sides of this road are a few trees. I had seen some old, broken glass in the sand, and this particular day I decided to dig. Sure enough, I found several old bottles hidden in the sand. Old foundations never cease to amaze me. If you look long enough and have the time, you will be successful.

As I was walking on another occasion, I heard noises off some distance in the forest. It sounded like a small child crying. As I continued to walk, I heard the noise or crying move up to the front of me close to the road. The crying became louder and nearer. The hair on my neck began to stand up. All of a sudden, a bobcat jumped out of a tree beside the road, looked at me, snarled, and then bounded off into the forest. A second cat crossed several yards further up the road. Yes, I was nervous. I figured the pair of bobcats were either hunting or mating. This was a first for me and I only wish I had had a camera.

I walked this route for about a year until my limp became less obvious. My leg continued to improve and is much better today! I can now walk for long distances without pain and once again go on long bottle digging adventures. Before I leave this area, the reader might be interested to know that these walks are very rewarding, enjoyable, and healthy. Look for an area in your neck of the woods that is off the beaten path. You will enjoy the adventures!

Old dumps are not always found out in the wilderness. For those of you who live in a metropolitan area, sometimes you only have to walk a short distance. A few years ago, my son was leaving the city of Waterville, Maine. He was aware of an old set of buildings that had burned. On this particular day, he had decided to search beside the main road. He pulled over, stopped, and began his search. McDonald's could be seen from where he was searching, and he was a couple hundred yards from Interstate 95.

Just beyond a clump of bushes, he found a ravine that appeared to have been dug out. Scratching around, he began to find 19th century bottles. Leaves were on bushes and trees so it probably was early summer. At any rate, since it was so close to the main road and nearby houses, he took a few bottles, came home, and asked if I would like to return. Silly Boy! We returned and filled several buckets with treasures.

This ravine was a reminder that you don't always have to travel great distances to locate old dumps. The key to locating this dump was knowing the general date of the old buildings that had been destroyed by fire. The buildings were part of a pre-victorian farm, and the foundation was on a hill overlooking the city of Waterville.

Returning from my walk one day, I had just driven out of the forest, and the people at the house opposite the old tote road were having a yard sale. Pulling in, I noticed a table with old bottles on display. These bottles were different; they were covered with barnacles. Upon inquiring, I found out the owner was a scuba diver. He had been to the ocean, and while diving, had found many old bottles. These bottles were beautiful; however, they were not cleaned. My son and I have no idea how to clean barnacles off bottles and neither did the owner. If the reader knows, please let us know at P.O. Box 615, Norridgewock, ME 04957.

Once before, I had met a young man who scuba-dived off the coast of Maine. He also had many bottles collected from the ocean and told me there were hundreds more still down there. He further said, "I could fill burlap bags full of bottles." I was interested and was supposed to meet him on a Saturday morning. We were going to fill some bags. He never showed up for our adventure; however, I'm convinced there are many bottles in the ocean for someone willing to scuba dive.

Every now and then I return to the world of Burger King, McDonald's, Kentucky Fried Chicken, and gas stations. The sameness is deafening. It isn't long before I succumb to urban fatigue. Once I was talking to a young African American from New York City. After a lengthy discussion, we arrived at some conclusions.

I had related to him that one night I arrived in New York City by Greyhound Bus from Nashville, Tennessee. It was late and I felt very uncomfortable getting off the bus at the terminal. I had to wait an hour for my next connection to Boston.

I looked around, saw a security station, and headed for what to me was protection. Being a simple country boy, I knew I was out of my league. Conversely, my African American friend had been with me headed for Oakland, Maine to look at a restored, one-room schoolhouse. He had just arrived in Maine and was trying to get adjusted, and as we left his home and started out, we almost struck a huge bull moose. His eyes became huge and he actually slid down in the car seat, not daring to look back out the window. He admitted that, in this instance, it was he who was out of his element.

The point of this is we agreed that I would be comfortable with him in New York City, and he would be comfortable with me in the Maine woods. We both learned a great lesson to not enter another person's domain unless you're knowledgeable. The fast track of the urban city is exciting and rewarding, but it is also crowded, noisy, dangerous, and reflects a sameness of activity. Your wallet is the best object for survival. On the other hand, in rural Maine, your compass is the best object for survival. A rural person walks the logs, where an urban person logs on. My only criticism is there are too many people who talk the talk, but don't walk the walk.

Mercer, Maine has a new bridge. It's built over a stream that runs out of Mercer Bog right through the middle of town. Years ago, an old dump was right beside the stream. It is now buried with the new bridge. My son got to the dump before the new bridge was constructed. He had to move huge pieces of granite to find bottles. The old bridge had a foundation of granite. The new bridge was constructed out of steel and concrete.

The town of Mercer was incorporated in the 18th century. Obviously, there were bottles dating back to the first settlers. On one occasion, I walked down a path leading to a pasture. The path followed the east side of Mercer Bog and terminated at a stonewall. In among the rocks were several treasures. I remember two of the bottles were medicine. One was embossed J.R. Nickles, Chemists, Boston. The other was embossed Schenck's Pulmonic Syrup, Philadelphia. Both are bottle glass green in color and were blown in a mold with applied lips. Each bottle has many bubbles in the glass. They adorn a shelf in my rumpus room and bring back wonderful memories.

Talking about the bridge, reminds me of the bridge in Canaan, Maine that crosses Route 2 in the center of town. On several occasions my son, a friend, and I have dug along the bank just below the bridge. Examples of wonderful blue, bulk inks were found. One was a pint, the other a quart. Both inks had spouts made into the applied lip. These two are in my son's curio cabinet for all to enjoy.

The town of Canaan is a very old town and very interesting. I'm looking forward to exploring a road called the Battle Ridge Road. I'm told this name came from a couple of families feuding like the Hatfield's and McCoy's. Many bottle hounds have dug in Canaan, as the evidence is very obvious. Like my son says, "Show me a dump that has been dug and I'll still find a bottle."

One day while walking along the west bank of the Kennebec River in Norridgewock, I found a vinegar cruet. It was natural glass with red swirls circling the base. This find triggered my digging instincts. Before I finished, several bottles were found including another cruet and a Dr. Hostetter's Bitters. This bank was visited many times by my family with great success. During the flood of 1987, the bank was washed away as the trees fell over, weakening the soil. It seems so strange to go up the river and look at the bank that once was covered with hemlock and other trees. Now the bank is cleared of trees, and all that remains is sand.

My boat has been such a pleasure. In the spring, I have gone up the Kennebec and returned with a mess of fiddleheads, several brown trout, and quite a lot of old bottles. One day I went up the river and stalled my motor on some eel traps. There was no way I could start the engine. It began to rain and I began to row. Two and a half hours later I found myself at the Norridgewock Boat Landing. Several days went by before I was ready for another boat trip. I've noticed the older one gets, the lamer one becomes.

At any rate, the fiddleheads, brown trout, and bottles were all picked, caught, and dug within a half mile of each other. Bomazeen Rips was the general location. In the spring, this section of the Kennebec is fished rather heavily. Later on in the season, the water becomes too warm for salmon and brown trout. Usually the chubs, suckers, and bass move in with the warm water, although fly fishing in the evening will produce a few salmon and brownies.

A dump is located a few hundred yards above the rips on the east shore. It has been dug out, but we won't tell my son, as I'm sure he will prove me a liar. It's remarkable to come home with my boat loaded with these three treasures. In a sense it's like winning the Triple Crown in horse racing.

My collection of bottles is loaded with old medicines. They probably were on the market from 1850 until the advent of the Pure Food and Drug Laws around the early part of the 20th century. At one time or other, each of us has seen on television the horse and wagon coming into town driven by a medicine man. Usually a medicine man put on some kind of show and expounded at great length to the value of his patent medicine. There were such medicine names like Lydia Pinkham, the Seven Sutherland Sisters, Wahoo Bitters, Dr. Clark's Compound Syrup of Wild Cherry & Tar, and Dr. Pierce's Pile Cure.

The list goes on and on with hundreds and hundreds of apothecary and other types of drugstore bottles. Most of mine are embossed and can be found listed in a good bottle book such as *The Bottle Book: A*

Comprehensive Guide to Historic, Embossed Medicine Bottles, by Richard E. Fike. There are so many in my collection, that a book would have to be published simply to list all of them. There are books on the market that simply do just that. I find them rather boring, and I use these books only for reference.

The next largest classification in my collection is whiskey. These are three-piece-mold whiskies; turn-in-the-mold whiskies; green, amber, clear, and black glass whiskies; and there are all sizes, from pints to quarts. Most are embossed with lettering or design. I'll name a few: an amber Hayner, Wright and Taylor; and there are several decanters and several bar bottles, such as Good Old Bourbon in a Hog's, and Duffy's Malt Whiskey. Again, the list goes on and on; I'll not bore the reader with a listing. One thing is for sure, our ancestors sure liked their whiskey. Most dumps always provide some sort of alcoholic beverage bottle.

As a bottle hound, I'm somewhat prejudiced. The purpose of this book, however, is to suggest to the reader to develop any hobby that can be enjoyed together as a family. A hobby hopefully will generate memories and ultimately facilitate communication. Any hobby will do as long as you're outdoors.

Bird watching is a hobby that is popular with many people. All you need is a pair of binoculars, unless you want to tape their song, or a camcorder to film their activity. Another hobby could be rock collecting. A collection of rocks is very nice to display. Again, this hobby is not expensive, as all you need is a rock chisel or hammer. There are many places throughout Maine to search for different rocks. Depending on your degree of interest, there are precious stones, as well as semi-precious. I have seen collections that are very valuable. Still, another hobby could be collecting insects, such as spiders, beetles, or flies. A collection of these creepy, crawly creatures would be never ending.

Going on trips to collect new samples for your hobby translates into adventures. Adventures for you and the family as well as friends can be exciting. The off season for these hobbies usually is during the winter months. This is the time to fine tune your display by arranging your samples while researching, writing, or doing whatever else is a necessary component of your hobby.

The not so obvious elements to any sort of collecting hobby are the adventures you have shared with someone else. It is most desirable to write these experiences down in a personal journal. Who knows, someday you might write a book, and this journal could then become invaluable.

The ultimate benefit to a hobbyist is not only the adventure or experience, but also the lasting memories between family and/or friends that can be talked about for years. It generates stories that bonds friends and families together, stories that are cherished, passed down through the years, and eventually become heirlooms. These stories become the thread that runs so true between father and son, as in my case, or between father and daughter, or any other combination of family and friends who were privileged to be together for a moment in time. So, whether it is bottle digging, being a rock hound, bird watching, or insect collecting, begin to think of a hobby that will help keep your family together.

Whatever your hobby, always be alert. Bottles can be found anywhere. One day I stopped at an old, deserted house. It actually was falling down. I climbed down through an old, rotten floor into the cellar. Sticking out of the old, dirt, cellar floor was a Duffy's Malt Liquor.

Keep your eyes peeled! You never know when you will be lucky. For example, one day I was walking out behind an old barn in the town of Canaan. The sun's rays struck some glass and glittered like a small mirror. In walking over to the spot, I found an old Pepper Sauce bottle, green in color, with swirls of glass in circles embossed on the bottle.

I have found bottles in many different ways. For example, I have simply walked along an old dirt road and found bottles. If you have friends who live in an old home, ask if you can look in their attic or maybe check out the old barn. Encourage anyone to bring bottles to you for identification. Most people could care less about an old bottle until they find out it may have value. If you're a good old Maine horse trader, a deal may be struck. Remember my son raking old leaves for that special bottle he gave me? Use your Maine ingenuity and you will be surprised at what you can accomplish.

A word to the wise: treat people honestly, sincerely, and with courtesy, and you will be rewarded!

Many people bring bottles to either my son or me for identification and end up giving them to us. I usually reciprocate by giving them a container of maple syrup or something that is of value to them. Watch yard sales. I have picked up a whole box full of bottles for next to nothing. At auctions I have experienced the same thing. I have bid a buck on a box of bottles and taken them home.

The history of the state of Maine really begins in the year 1820. Preceding this year, Maine was a district owned by the state of Massachusetts. This was a district overrun by Native Americans, and later there was a period in history known as the French and Indian War.

Once Massachusetts cleaned up their north woods wilderness, towns had already begun to incorporate, and this continued at a rapid pace. The Southern part of the state began to incorporate in the early 1700's. The further north one travels the newer the town. When Massachusetts was partitioned by the district of Maine to become a state, the partition requested the city of Portland become its capital. Along with statehood, this was granted. It wasn't until years later that Augusta was selected as the new capital of the state of Maine.

In early years, present day Augusta was know as Cushnoc. Sometimes I wonder if the War of 1812 had something to do with this change of capital names. History reflects how the British bombarded Portland and literally burned the city to the ground. Many of the people from burned-out Portland moved or were displaced far inland about 100 miles, and the town of New Portland was incorporated. Also at that time, it may have been that Cushnoc was considered a better location for a capital. Cushnoc was 50 miles further inland and on a river. Off Portland Harbor during the War of 1812, the British anchored their ships and simply lobbed their shells into the city, creating huge fires. By moving the capital inland, this devastation never happened again. So, Cushnoc was renamed Augusta, and it was created as the new capital of Maine.

Much of the architecture of Augusta is Federalist. In fact the so-called Old Federalist Road can still be traced from Augusta to Winslow. My son and I have walked many miles of this old road and found many bottle treasures. The closer one stays to the east shore of the Kennebec River the more successful your adventure will be.

It's interesting to note how influential the river was on settlements. The river was the first means of transportation, and small neighborhoods sprang up along its banks. If you follow the Old Federalist Road, these neighborhoods become more prevalent. Many dumps were located in ravines or gullies that pitch east to west into the Kennebec River. Farmers apparently dumped their trash over the banks of these gullies. Later in the 19th century, the railroad also followed the river's course. Today, the main road from Augusta to Winslow bypasses most of the Old Federalist Road.

I shall return to this area of the state this summer. There are treasures to be found and sights to experience. This old road rings of Maine history. After all, Native Americans, trappers, and colonists walked these paths from Fort Western in Cushnoc to Fort Halifax in Winslow. This path became known as the Old Federalist Road, and it is a bottle digger's paradise. It must be remembered that this old road was also used by stagecoach. Heading north on this old road, travelers connected with the Old Canada Road.

One day I drove down by the Kennebec River at the riverside just north of Augusta and walked a short distance down the railroad tracks. I came to a granite bridge that crossed a small brook carrying the railroad tracks. As I moved along, history came alive under my feet. Moving under some trees, thoughts of the extreme hardship the settlers of this land came to my mind. Men who constructed this granite bridge must have been remarkable. The hardships they endured were tremendous. How did they get to work? Did they live in tents? Was the granite shipped down the river or was it hauled by oxen? Where were their homes and families? These are just a few questions that ran through my mind.

It reminded me of the hardships that my stepfather-in-law and grandfather once told me about. They told me what it was like when they worked in the woods at the turn of the 20th century. These men traveled north from their homes and families into the Maine wilderness to work at logging operations. They left in the fall and returned to their loved ones in the spring. They lived in barracks, ate in a mess hall, and worked from sun-up to sundown. After working hard all day, grandfather indicated at night when the men took their socks off, it was rather smelly. In the mess hall, the bull cook was boss. Whatever he said in the mess hall was law. These men were hungry and never argued with the "Bull," as he was affectionately called. In later years, this was a carryover to school cafeterias, if a teacher shouted, "Lumberjack," children automatically quieted down.

The men who built the railroad must have experienced similar hardships. How did they live? I wonder if they went home on weekends? Did they live on small farms?

In Fairfield there is an area called the Ohio Hill Road. It derived its name from farmers finally giving up and moving to the state of Ohio. Farming was just too difficult in Maine to make a living. Ohio was richer farming country and without the rocks. At any rate, these men built the Maine Railroad. From my point of view, they must have suffered heartache, backaches, and headaches.

As I sat there contemplating, it dawned on me that across the river was the town of Sidney. The old road that passed by the cemetery leading down to the west side of the river may have been leading to a field across the river. This was the road close to "The Dump," in Sidney. Later, I was to learn that indeed the old road did lead travelers across the riverside in both summer and winter.

The town of Sidney revealed several more old dumps. They were not as rich as "The Dump," but treasures were extracted. Several unembossed bottles are displayed in my curio cabinet from one particular dump. Also, my first umbrella ink was found in the same trash. This was an area off the River Road, almost into Augusta. We noticed an old foundation close to a local residence. Stopping at the residence, we asked permission to scout around his property. The owner allowed us permission and we were off on another adventure.

We walked out back of the foundation through the woods and the tall swale grass, and eventually we came to a knoll. There had been old trash dumped over the knoll, so we began to scratch and dig. We began to turn up bottle after bottle that we found about a foot beneath the surface. Many of these bottles had open pontils.

Nothing will generate energy in a bottle hound more than finding bottles. The better the bottle the more the energy. We spent the afternoon digging and eventually went home with quite a few treasures.

It should be pointed out, for every dump with bottles, the next eight might come up with not a single treasure. In such cases, the only treasure would be the adventure of hunting for the dump. At times, sharing experiences are more valuable than finding a bottle. For example, once I stepped into a hornets' nest and was peppered with bites. On another occasion, a huge snake came slithering out of the hole in which I was digging. Snakes bother me, and as I remember, my digging was done for the day. Usually, though, the experiences become fond memories to share over the long winter months, as well as over the years.

MESSAGE IN A BOTTLE

This hobby of bottle digging is contagious. From my experience, bottle hounds who are in this hobby for enjoyment stay the course, meaning, of course, that the joy keeps the interest alive. Maybe it's more than joy, though, as sometimes the amount of work involved to hunt, dig, locate, and excise the bottles far exceeds the treasure. Many times the endurance, sweat, and aching muscles bring into question the sanity of a bottle digger.

Back in the 1960's, when every third person was a bottle digger, the hobby could be called more of a vocation than a hobby. Many of these diggers were in the hobby for money. At that time there was a market for antique bottles. I'm told truckloads of bottles left the state for the south and west. These bottles were destined for flea markets, auctions, and antique shops. The digger-for-profit expected to go out on a Sunday afternoon and make a few bucks.

There's nothing wrong with this idea except it finally became self-defeating. The profit digger would not put the necessary time and effort into his/her endeavors; if the bottle couldn't be found quickly, the procedure was to move on to other locations. Greed seemed to be the motivator. On the other hand, the true bottle hound is in no hurry. Time is on the hound's side, and energy, perseverance; and stamina are the hound's tools. The treasures (bottles) are not for sale. They are for enjoyment, and the excursion or adventure is as important as the bottle.

Each bottle in a true bottle hound's collection has a story to tell and, therefore, a memory to be treasured.

As I look at my collection, memories flood my mind like a personal diary or journal. I'm able to recall many fond adventures. I'm pleased to say that these adventures were shared with my dearest friends, family, and neighbors.

In this book, I have tried to trace thirty years of enjoyment and experience for the reader. From 1971 through the beginning of the new millennium, a sizable span of my life has been shared. My fondest hope is that the experiences in this book will foster bottle digging as a hobby, a hobby for others to enjoy and share in the environmental wonders of tramping the Maine wilderness.

Perhaps the new breed of "bottle hounds" will bring pieces of broken bottles home and use them in artistic showpieces. For example, pieces of glass of various colors could be embedded in a medium such as plaster of paris. A collage could be the result, or maybe the base of a lamp could be shaped out of it. The author has other unique ideas to bring to fruition that could be made using pieces of broken bottles.

Another idea is to collect a bottle from each of the towns in Maine. My present collection has approximately 100 separate bottles with different Maine towns embossed in the glass. Maybe just a collection of Bitters bottles would be the reader's desire. Or, a collection of medicinal bottles, or any other category would be the reader's desire. Let your imagination be your guide as you begin your hobby.

Old maps may be helpful in your interest. If so, go to your local County Registry of Deeds Office for photocopies. The real old maps trace the old country roads and other historical areas of the county or state.

For those of you who might be interested, the state of Maine has 33,000 square miles. I haven't scratched the surface of this area. From Aroostock County and Fort Kent in the north, to Lincoln County and Fort Edgecomb in the south, from Washington County and Campobello Island in the east, and from Oxford County and the White Mountain National Forest in the west, there are adventures and treasures to be enjoyed by everyone. Take your family or friends out this next weekend to hunt for old bottles; maybe just maybe I'll see you on my next adventure. Good luck and may all your adventures end with treasures and memories to think about over the years.

BIBLIOGRAPHY

Calvert, Mary R. *The Kennebec Wilderness Awakens.* Lewiston: Twin City Printery, 1986.

Fike, Richard E. *The Bottle Book: A Comprehensive Guide to Historic, Embossed Medicine Bottles.* Salt Lake City: Smith, 1987.

Hubka, Thomas C. *Big House, Little House, Back House, Barn: The Connected Farm Buildings of New England.* Hanover: UP of New England, 1984.

Kovel, Ralph and Terry. *Kovels' Bottles Price List.* 11th ed. New York: Random, 1999.

McKearin, Helen, and Kenneth M. Wilson. *American Bottles and Flasks and Their Ancestry.* New York: Crown Publishers, 1978.

Thoreau, Henry David. *The Maine Woods.* New York: Penguin, 1988.

Index of Maine Towns

Augusta	89		Lexington	89
Bangor	48		Lisbon	54
Bath	48		Lowelton	97
Bingham	37		Madison	50
Bowerbank	68		Mercer	76
Canaan	132		Norridgewock	35
Concord	89		Oakland	23
Cornville	103		Orono	5
Emden	89		Philips	60
Enchanted	89		Pierce Pond	
Fairfield Center	93		Township	89
Fairfield	5, 89		Pleasant Ridge	89
Farmington	44		Rangeley	48
Farmington	5, 44		Sidney	39
Freeman	60		Skinner	97
Greenville	48		Skowhegan	49
Hinckley	105		Solon	89
Industry	40		Starks	37
Johnson			Waterville	129
Mountain	89		West Forks	89
Larone	30		Winslow	89
Lewiston	88			

www.ingramcontent.com/pod-product-compliance
Lightning Source LLC
Chambersburg PA
CBHW032124090426
42743CB00007B/461